MONDOFRAGILE PRESENTS

MASCOTTE!

SELECTED BY DELICATESSEN

© Yuka Morii

happy books

www.mondofragile.com

MASCOTTE!
selected by Delicatessen

Happy Books, Italy
ISBN 88-86416-48-2

Concept:
cristiana valentini & gabriele fantuzzi
www.delicatessen.it

Art direction:
gabriele fantuzzi , delicatessen
gabriele@delica.it

Distribution:
www.happybookstore.com
happy@happybooks.it

Website:
www.mondofragile.com

Contact:
info@mondofragile.com

Mascotte! © 2003 First published in Italy
by Happy Books srl

this page: Jean-Marie Angles
Autoportrait

right page: Genevieve Gauckler
Sipher

printed and bound in Italy by
Grafiche Jolly - Modena

INDEX

Prolegomeni: *buona fortuna*

matteo bittanti

Mascotte: sostantivo femminile, "persona, animale o oggetto usato come portafortuna"

Francesi, per la precisione provenzali, le origini di "mascotte".
È nel sud della Francia infatti che si diffonde, nell'Ottocento, il termine "ma-scoto" traducibile come 'oggetto di magia, sortilegio, amuleto'. "Mascoto" è il diminutivo di "masco", 'strega'. Come dire: il legame tra l'oggetto e la dimen-sione dell'occulto è già evidente a livello etimologico. Non solo: "masco", a sua volta, deriva dal latino "masca", ovvero fantasma.

Gli spettri si aggirano per il mondo: mascotte, pupazzi, marionette e avatar di ogni forma e dimensione si materializzano sugli schermi dei nostri computer, delle televisioni e dei telefonini. Nessuna sorpresa: come ha dimostrato Sconce (2000), gli ectoplasmi infestano i media, vecchi e nuovi. Internet, in partico-lare, è uno straordinario generatore e diffusore di creature fantasmatiche: l'ultima conferma arriva dall'angosciante *Kaïro* (2001) di Kurosawa, (Kyoshi, non Akira).

La mascotte è una creatura liminale, che oscilla tra il mondo materiale e la dimensione soprannaturale, tra il tangibile e l'etereo. Rappresenta il punto di intersezione tra l'umano e il divino. La sua liminalità è performante e pertur-bante assieme. È grazie a una piéce teatrale di Edmond Audran (1842-1901), intitolata non a caso, "La Mascotte" (1880), che il termine entra a far parte del linguaggio comune. L'operetta racconta le tragicomiche disavventure di una ragazza di campagna che porta "fortuna" a chiunque la "possieda". Nella migliore tradizione della commedia degli equivoci, questo sorprendente potere è efficace solo nella misura in cui la ragazza riesce a conservare la sua verginità...

...E qui arriviamo alla terza caratteristica della mascotte: la purezza e l'in-nocenza, due elementi che rinviano a loro volta ad un immaginario simbolico tipicamente infantile. Ne consegue che il modello estetico di riferimento della mascotte è quello del *kawaii*, uno stile che, come ha osservato Go-marasca (2001), "nasce nel momento in cui la *shojo bunka* (la cultura degli adolescenti) si incontra con la cultura euro-americana del *cute*, l'estetica del ludico infantile importata in Giappone dall'Occidente" (p. 68). Il *kawaii*, secondo Shimamura (citato in Gomarasca, 2001, pp. 61) si caratterizza per la presenza di quattro attributi: per il suo essere "piccolo, innocente, tenero e rotondeggiante". Questi elementi informano l'iconografia della maggior parte delle mascotte raccolte in questo libro (la spigolosità sopravvive in pochi au-tori occidentali — penso ai pupazzi meccanici dell'americano Ian Stokes o ai "plastibi" di Jean-Marie Angles — la malvagità nelle figure del messicano Paco Aguayo, ma nel complesso dominano le figure placide e globulose). Un'icono-grafia fatta di appendici tentacolari, teste gigantesche, sorrisi beati e occhio-ni sognanti. Un'estetica zuccherosa, floscia e morbida, a metà tra il kitsch e la fiaba, il videogioco e l'illustrazione per bambini.
Un'estetica più volte irrisa, ma mai veramente compresa.

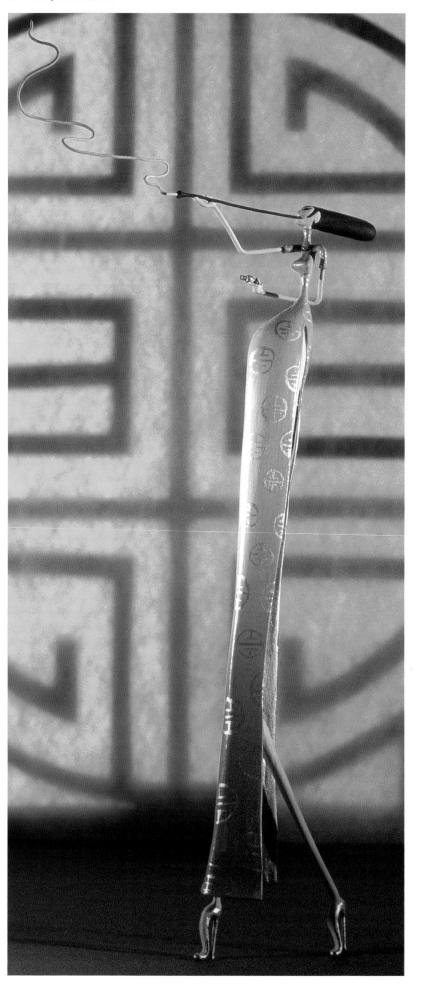

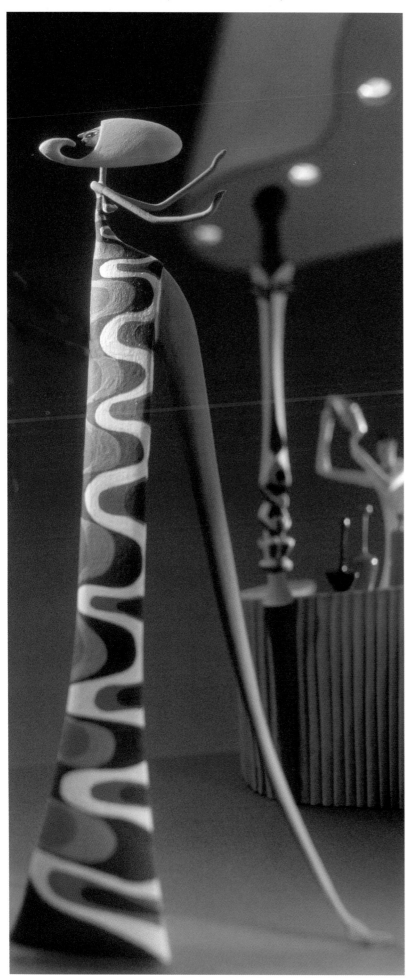

Prolegomena: *good luck*

matteo bittanti

Mascot: a person, animal, or object adopted by a group as a symbolic figure especially to bring them good luck

"Mascot" has a French soul. The term comes from the Provençal *"mascoto"*, which means "magic artifact, charm, talisman". Moreover, *"mascoto"* is the diminutive of *masco*, which can be roughly translated as "witch". In other words, the intimate relationship between the mascot and the uncanny is clear even at the etymological level. If we need a further proof, *masco* comes from Medieval Latin *masca*, "phantom"<u>or</u>"ghost".

No wonder, then, that specters are haunting the world: mascots, puppets, dolls, and avatars materialize on our computer screens, televisions and cellular phone displays. No surprises here: Sconce (2000) proved that ghosts and ectoplasms literally possess our media, old and new. Internet, in particular, seems to be the most powerful generator and diffuser of phantasmatic creatures. One does not need to Kurosawa's (Kyoshi, not Akira) disturbing *Kaïro* (2001) to convince himself.

Mascots are liminal creatures. They oscillate between the material and the supernatural worlds, between the tangible and the ethereal. They represent the point of intersection between the mundane and the divine. The mascot's liminal quality is both a performance and a perturbation. According to some historians, the term's popularity is intimately connected with Edmond Audran's (1842-1901) play, "La Mascotte" (1880). Although it was first used in the first half of 19th century, the word *"mascotte"* became common only after Audran's operetta about a young girl, who, if she remains a virgin will bring good luck and fortune to whom she comes in contact.

This leads us to the third attribute of the mascot: purity and innocence. These two elements belong to the symbolic imagery of childhood. No wonder, then its aesthetic frame of reference is that of *kawaii*. A style that, according to Gomarasca (2001), kawaii "was born when *shojo bunka* (the teenager culture) met the Euro-American culture of 'cuteness', the infantile, playful aesthetics that Japan imported from the West" (p. 68) Shimamura adds that *kawaii*'s essential traits are "smallness, innocence, tenderness, and roundness" (quoted in Gomarasca, 2001, p. 61). These elements inform the iconography of the vast majority of the mascots that appear on these pages (The antithesis of *kawaii, kowai*, the frightening element can only be found in Paco Aguaios' creatures, and the only exception to the otherwise pervasive roundness is found in the works of Ian Stokes and Jean-Marie Angle). This iconography is replete with tentacles and weird appendixes, huge heads, placid smiles, plump and soft shapes, and dreamy eyes. A syrupy style that borrows elements from videogames, fables, and *manga*. Often derided, this aesthetic has never been fully understood, let alone appreciated for what it represents.

If France is the home country of the mascot – at least on an etymological level – Japan is its promised land. Nippon designers have been using the new electronic medium to reshape old myths for quite a while now. After all, mascots are an

falling in love.

Se la Francia è la patria – quantomeno etimologica – della mascotte, il Giappone è la sua terra promessa. La attesta l'opera instancabile dei designer nipponici, che si servono del medium elettronico per dare nuove forme a vecchi miti. La mascotte, infatti, appartiene di diritto alla storia (e preistoria) della cultura popolare di questa nazione. I suoi antesignani sono le bambola *daruma* e *fushimi ningyo* (Gerbert, 2001). La prima è un giocattolo-talismano, capace di scacciare la sfortuna e le malattie. Dipinta di rosso amaranto, il colore preferito del demone del vaiolo, la bambola *daruma* è l'incarnazione del leggendario monaco buddista Bodhidharma. L'amuleto ludico veniva collocato sui cuscini dei bambini al fine di proteggere il loro sonno. La *daruma* è rotonda e priva di arti: stando alla leggenda, Bodhidharma aveva meditato così a lungo che le appendici corporee gli erano divenute ormai di impaccio più che di aiuto. Secondo l'usanza nipponica, ogni Capodanno un bambino esprime un desiderio e disegna una pupilla alla bambola. Se il desiderio si avvera, il ragazzino non deve fare altro che pitturare anche il secondo occhio e disfarsi della bambola entro il Capodanno successivo. Una funzione analoga veniva svolta dalla *fushimi ningyo*, la bambola-talismano in vendita nel Santuario di Fushimi Inari a Tokyo, capace di portare felicità e fortuna a chiunque l'avesse ricevuta in dono. Ma la mascotte *par excellence* è l'onnipresente gattino portafortuna, autentico antesignano di Hello Kitty.

Le mascotte sono delle icone. La radice del termine è greca: *eikon*, dal verbo *eikenai*, "assomigliare". L'icona è l'immagine - ma anche il veicolo - del divino e del sacro. È un emblema. Un simbolo. È un termine del gergo informatico e videoludico. Nella mascotte coesistono tutte queste differenti accezioni. Dietro alla sua apparenza di *nonsense*, la mascotte addensa in sé una pluralità di sensi, fino a creare dissenso. La mascotte, al pari dell'icona religiosa, evoca un immaginario che non possiede in proprio e rimanda ad un'alterità misteriosa e affascinante. La mascotte è sacra e profana assieme.

Le mascotte sono degli idoli. La radice del termine è greca: *eidolon*: 'fantasma' (ancora!), ma anche 'ideale'. Oggetto di culto e di devozione, ma anche falsa divinità. È una forma priva di consistenza ontologica. Le mascotte possiedono tutti i caratteri dell'*eidolon* descritti nel Salmo 115: sono "opera di mani umane. Hanno bocche, ma non parlano. Hanno occhi, ma non vedono. Hanno orecchie, ma non odono. Hanno nasi, ma non odorano. Hanno mani, ma non toccano. Hanno piedi, ma non camminano, e neppure parlano con la loro gola. Coloro che li fabbricano saranno simili a loro, e così ognuno che in essi confidi." Ne consegue che il *graphic designer* è un idolo. Ne consegue che i suoi estimatori sono degli idoli. Cosa significa tutto ciò? Ci viene in aiuto Marshall McLuhan (1964), secondo il quale "la contemplazione degli idoli, o l'uso della tecnologia, conforma gli uomini ad essi" (p.55). Non c'è scampo.

Le mascotte sono dei feticci. Il culto per la mascotte presenta tutti i caratteri del feticismo. L'oggetto-immagine si carica di un'aura di misticismo che esige rispetto. Il feticcio attesta la forza travolgente, seducente, destabilizzante dell'oggetto-immagine e dell'immagine-oggetto sullo spettatore. Il feticcio resiste ai processi di strumentalizzazione. Esiste e resiste all'urgenza pragmatica. Di fronte alla legittima domanda "che cos'è? a cosa serve?", la mascotte si limita ad osservarci in modo beffardo. E a ridere. Di gusto.

Intermezzo cinematografico. Secondo la mitologia nipponica, la bambola conserva e veicola l'anima di chi la possiede. Assume connotati onirici, a volte rassicuranti, a volte inquietanti. Il secondo episodio di *Sogni* (*Dreams*, 1990) di Kurosawa (Akira, non Kyoshi) ha come protagonista un ragazzino che scopre la vita misteriosa e affascinante nascosta in un pescheto apparentemente morto. In una memorabile sequenza, quindici bambole imperiali viventi, identiche nella forme a quelle che la sorella del protagonista tiene in bella mostra nella sua stanza, danno vita ad un affascinante

integral part of their culture. Their precursors are the *daruma* and the *fushimi ningyo* dolls (Gerbert, 2001). A *daruma* is toy-talisman, believed to act as a charm to avert evil and bring good fortune. Painted red, the favorite color of the smallpox demon, these legless and armless tumbler dolls represented the legendary Buddhist saint, Bodhidharma. They were set by the pillows of childre serving as propitiatory talismans to curry favor with and ward off the demons. The *fushimi ningyo* doll was thought to possess prophylactic powers and was used to ward off disease and misfortune. Sold to pilgrims at the Fushimi Inari Shrine in Kyoto that they might share the shrine deity's blessings with those who stayed at home, it became a staple. In addition, a flotilla of lucky charm cats used by Japanese merchants transported good luck from one place to another, to attract customers and to insure success in business. In other words, *Hello Kitty* did not really invent anything new.

Mascots are icons. The term comes from Greek *eikOn,* from *eikenai*, "to resemble". An icon is a pictorial representation, typically, a religious image painted on a small wooden panel and used in the devotions of Eastern Christians. The term has a negative connotation: often it is used to define objects of uncritical devotion. Icons are also graphic symbols on a computer display screen which suggests the purpose of an available function. The mascot comprises all these meanings: it's both esoteric and functional, ancient and ultra-modern. Behind its apparent nonsense, the mascot condenses a plurality of meanings. Just like the religious icon, the mascot evokes

an "Outer" dimension that does not own. The mascot is simultaneously sacred and profane.

Mascots are idols. The term comes from Greek *eidolon* which stands for 'image', 'ghost' (again!) but also "ideal". An idol is a representation or symbol of an object of worship. It is not hard to notice the negative connotation: idols are often regarded as false gods. And yet, they are objects of extreme devotion. It is a pure appearance that seeks for substance. In the "gadget-lover" chapter of *Understanding media*, McLuhan (1964) recalls the 115th Psalm: "Their idols are silver and gold, the work of men's hands. They have mouths, but they speak not; eyes have they, but they see not: They have ears, but they hear not; Noses have they, but they smell not: They have hands, but they handle not: feet have they, but they walk not: neither speak they through their throat. They that make them are like unto them; *so is* every one that trusteth in them." To contemplate idols — which, in McLuhan's terminology equals to "using technology" — makes humans similar to idols. There is no way out.

Mascots are fetishes. Material objects believed to have magical power to protect or aid its owner. Their mystic aura demands respect. The fetish is a sign of the overwhelming and seductive power of the object-image and the image-object. The fetish resists functionality. Its existence is paradoxical. When we ask ourselves "what is it? What is it for?" the mascot just looks at us, smiling and laughing. Laughing out loud.

Cinematic intermission. In Japanese mythology, the doll is a soul bearer. It is linked to the dream world: it can both reassure and scare us. The second fragment of Akira Kurosawa's *Dreams* (*Yume*, 1990) has a little boy who is lured into an orchard, where he is confronted by the spirits of the trees, which have taken the form of fifteen giant living ceramic dolls. We encounter more dolls in Takeshi Kitano's masterpiece, Dolls (2002) which opens in media res with the traditional Japanese puppetry of Bunraku. Here the puppets — and puppified human beings - are the protagonists. Unlike Kurosawa's, these mascots bring despair and anguish rather than joy and luck. Cyborgs — the latest incarnation of the doll — appear in Mamoru Oshii's *Ghost in the Shell* (**Kôkaku kidôtai,** 1995), as a metaphor for the extinction of free will in the information society. The movie deals with an evil "Puppet master" who pulls the strings as he pleases. In all these examples, the doll embodies the perverse exchange between the living and the artificial, the human and the simulation. It subjugates man and traps him into the realm of the fantastic. The doll disguised as fetish, as Marx and Freud realized many years ago, is the manifestation of a pathology:.

Mascots are monsters that can't scare us. The creatures of *Monsters Inc.* (2001) try their best to terrify us. Instead, the make us laugh. Fact is: we live in a gigantic Monstropolis: the separation between the mundane and the supernatural is no longer valid. We are our enemies. We are our own monsters. Rather than a moral parable, *Monsters Inc.* is an aesthetics lesson: the "cute" design of its characters crushed the photorealistic ambitions of *Final Fantasy: The Spirits Within* (2001). It shares the *kawaii* imperative can also be found in the Pokémon monsters and in the creatures that inhabit Miyazaki's enchanted city (see *Spirited Away*, **Sen to Chihiro no kamikakushi**, 2001). The mascot combines the exoticism of the "other" with the reassuring familiarity of the anthropomorphic, nullifying violence and eroticism. The mascots — cinematographic and virtual — embody the man's ludic dimension. On that Lacanian mirror that is the computer screen, they reflect our aspirations to levity in an era of bacteriological warfare, terrorism and pre-emptive strikes. Instead of dismissing this phenomenon as "regressive", "unsettling" or simply "stupid", we understand the mascot fad (movement?) as an aesthetic answer to a nihilistic ethics.

danza che risveglia, per pochi interminabili istanti, il pescheto appassito. Ancora bambole, ma intese come fonte di disperazione anziché di gioia, compaiono nell'ultima splendida opera di Takeshi Kitano, *Dolls* (2002). Da mere comparse a protagoniste: le marionette mettono in scena un testo di Chikamatsu Monzaemon, "Meido no Hikyaku" ("I Messi dell'Inferno"). Il film si apre *in media res*, in un teatro del *bunraku*, una forma di teatro di marionette che risale al XVI secolo in cui il marionettista è in scena assieme al narratore-cantante e al suonatore di *tayu* e muove il suo grande pupazzo, dagli abiti ampi e colorati e dal volto bianco e inespressivo, secondo ritmi lenti e studiatissimi. Bambole (cyborg) ricorrono anche nel capolavoro *cyberpunk* di Mamoru Oshii, *Ghost in the Shell* (1995), una penetrante riflessione sul tema del libero arbitrio della società dell'informazione. Il cattivo della situazione è un fantomatico "Signore dei Pupazzi" che muove i fili a piacimento. In tutti questi casi, la bambola opera uno scambio perverso tra il vivente ed il non vivente: soggioga l'umano e lo imprigiona nell'antro del fantastico. La bambola-feticcio è, come avevano già intuito Marx e Freud, la manifestazione di una patologia, di una devianza.

Le mascotte sono mostri che non fanno paura. I protagonisti di *Monsters & Co.* (2001), vorrebbero terrorizzarci, ma finiscono per farci sorridere. Perché ormai viviamo in una gigantesca Monstropolis: la scissione tra la dimensione mondana e quella mostruosa è orma venuta a mancare. Ma *Monsters & Co.* è, prima di tutto, una lezione di estetica: al fallimento commerciale di *Final Fantasy: The Spirits Within* (2001) fa da contro altare il trionfo del "cute": penso alle bestiole di Pokémon, ma anche alle creature spaventose e tenere allo stesso tempo popolano la città incantata di Miyazaki (*Spirited Away*, 2001). Le mascotte coniugano l'esotismo del diverso alla rassicurante familiarità dell'antropomorfo, annullando ogni accenno erotico e violento. Le mascotte — cinematografiche e virtuali — incarnano il lato ludico, ma non sudicio, dell'essere umano, riflettono su quello specchio lacaniano che è lo schermo del computer i nostri desideri di spensieratezza nell'era della guerra preventiva, della minaccia batteriologica, dell'incubo del terrorismo. Lungi dal considerare questo fenomeno regressivo, inquietante o semplicemente stupido, ci limitiamo a prendere atto che le mascotte rappresentano una risposta estetica ad un'etica nichilista.

Intermezzo letterario. La bambola attraversa la narrativa nipponica. Ricorre spesso negli scritti di Junichiro Tanizaki, nella quale il pupazzo diventa in molti casi un surrogato dell'amore. Nel racconto "Il segreto" (Himitsu, 1911), Tanizaki racconta la storia di un uomo in cerca di solitudine, che finisce per innamorarsi di una bambola

Meomi Design /*Wallpaper*

di plastica, costruita ad immagine e somiglianza di un'attrice famosa. Anche ne *Gli insetti preferiscono le ortiche* (*Tade kuu mushi*, 1928-29), il protagonista, Kaname, si innamora di una donna-bambola, Ohisa ("eterna"). A poco a poco, il mondo di Kaname finisce per trasformarsi in una sorta di casa di bambole gigantesca. Fuori dal Giappone, si pensi alla forza di quell'icona pop che è Barbie. La ritroviamo in autori tanto diversi come Philip K. Dick (*Perky Pat*) e A.M. Homes (*Una vera bambola*). Secondo Kitti Carriker (1998), la bambola sintetizza le molteplicità disperse dell'uomo e, come tale, assurge a veicolo di nostalgia per un passato pre-moderno che "non è mai esistito se non sotto forma di narrativa" (p.27). Detto altrimenti, l'uomo idolatra la mascotte, la bambola e il feticcio perché anela all'unità.

Le mascotte sono, per definizione, minuscole. Come abbiamo precisato in apertura, "Mascoto" è un diminutivo di "Masco". Ora, cos'è, il diminutivo se non una forma di *rimpicciolimento*? Le mascotte sono delle vere e proprie miniature che vivono sui nostri computer. Sono creature lillipuziane che si muovono sulla superficie dello schermo. Si prestano volentieri alle nostre manipolazioni e soggiacciono docilmente ai nostri capricci. Esaltano il senso di onnipotenza del loro padrone, ma al tempo stesso lasciano intendere che potrebbero sottrarsi al suo controllo in qualunque momento, come i Fornit di quel celebre racconto di King (1985), "La ballata della pallottola flessibile".

La mascotte è un'icona della cultura di massa, tanto in Giappone quanto in occidente. È causa ed effetto dei processi di globalizzazione della *visual culture*, sospesa com'è tra favola e mercificazione. La mascotte è una visione fantasmatizzata del reale. Pur essendo una creatura dell'inconscio, è sempre e comunque accolta e incorporata nell'io. La mascotte vive di contaminazioni ed è, a sua volta, contaminante. Galleggia tra manga e videogames, *graphic design* e fumetto d'autore, *virtual pets* e robottini. La sua logica è inclusiva, non esclusiva.

L'invasione delle ultramascotte. La mascotte genera una pletora di gadget. Partecipare al suo variopinto mondo significa sperimentare l'acquisto impulsivo di oggetti fisici: la calcolatrice kawaii (immaginaria) di Ken Hoshino, le borse di plastilina di Mamiko Hasebe, le t-shirt e i portacellulari di Meomi Design, le bamboline del tedesco Boris Hoppek, gli occhialoni di Tinoland... Il gadget-mascotte si diffonde con la rapidità di un virus, contaminando chiunque ne entri in contatto. Ci tornano in mente

Literary intermission. Dolls are a recurrent motif in Japanese narrative. It is also one of Junic'hiro Tanizaki's obsessions. In his stories, the doll often represents a love surrogate. The protagonist in the bizarre love story, "the Secret"("Himitsu", 1911) becomes entangled with a plastic doll that resembles a popular actress. A similar theme can be found in "Some prefer nettles" (*Tade kuu mushi*, 1928-29). Here, a man called Kaname falls in love with a doll-like woman, Ohisa (literally, "eternal"). Little by little, his world implodes and turns into a dollhouse (a madhouse?). Even outside Japan, the doll dominates the most heterogeneous forms of narrative. Barbie, in particular, pops up in Philip K. Dick's stories (under the nom de plum of 'Perky Pat') and A.M. Homes' (see, for instance, "A real doll", one of the most absurd short stories in "The Safety of Objects"). According to Kitti Carriker (1998), the doll synthesises man's fragmented identities and thus, it becomes a vehicle for nostalgia for a pre-modern past that "did not exist if not as a form of fantasy" (p. 27). In other words, man idolizes the mascot, the doll and the fetish, because he aspires to become one.

Mascots are, by definition, tiny. As we pointed out at the beginning, "mascoto" is a diminutive of "masco". Now, a diminutive is just another word for "miniature". As Stewart (1993) noted, "The toy world presents a projection of the world of everyday life; this real world is miniaturized or giganticized in such a way as to test the relation between materiality and meaning" (p. 57) Mascot are little creatures that inhabit our computers. They are Lilliputian beings that move on the surface of the screen. They are easily manipulated. The exalt man's aspiration for omnipotence but, at the same time, let us know that they could betray us any second. They are like the Fornits, the mysterious creatures that we first met in Stephen King's "The Ballad of the Flexible

Bullet" (1985).

Mascots are popular culture icons. Both in Japan and in the Western world. It is both the cause and the outcome of the globalization processes imposed by an increasingly homogeneous visual culture. A culture that lies at the intersection of fairy tales and fabled commodities. Although the mascot is generated by the subconscious, it dominates the world of the "ego". It was born out of a plague. And it is highly contagious itself. It floats in a sea of videogames, *graphic design* e comic books, *virtual pets* and robot toys. Its logic is inclusive, not exclusive.

The invasion of the mascot-snatchers. The mascot generates a plethora of gadgets. To live its world require impulse buying and useless gizmos: the (imaginary) pocket calculator design by ken Hoshino, clay bags by Mamiko Hasebe, t-shirts and cell phone holders by Meomi Design, paper dolls made by Boris Hoppek, comic book spectacles by Tinoland... The gadget-mascot is like a deadly virus. Both Baudelaire and Benjiamin (Benjamin) talked about the "phantasmagoria of objects". In recent times, Gomarasca & Valtorta (1996), wrote that "*kawaii* is, above all, a market. A series of items produced by the industry of the "cute": gadgets, dolls, mascots, backpacks, notebooks, posters, t-shirts, food [...] Items that seem to belong to a plump and mellifluous world, a world on infantilism that, for some reasons, has a powerful appeal on Japanese teenagers and even grown-ups" (p. 71). One is left wondering if after Murakami and his "superflat" movement the distinction between art and gadget is still meaningful.

So far, so close. Just like Pokémon and Tamagotchi, the mascot is a catalyst of affection. Mascot fans gather in tribes that idolize the image-object. Their behaviour is both collective and ritual. Mascots are a cultural artefact but also a cult phenomenon. They lie at the intersection between process of hybridization between Western and Eastern cultures. They are bizarre, weird yet strangely familiar. Their visual language is both comforting and arcane. Far from being loved by a niche, the mascots have an enormous fan base. They occupy our times and spaces: think about Meomi Design's cute calendars... Think about Genevieve Gauckler's puppets that reinvented the zodiac but also the urban and suburban spaces.... Think about Boris Hoppek's surreal

Hiroshi Yoshii

le riflessioni di Baudelaire e Benjiamin sulla "fantasmagoria degli oggetti", ma anche le osservazioni di Gomarasca & Valtorta (1996), "Il *kawaii* è innanzitutto un mercato. Un'intera linea di articoli sfornati ogni stagione dall'industria del "cariiino": gadget, bambole, mascotte, cartelle, diari, poster, vestiti, cibi [...] Oggetti che rimandano ad un immaginario infantile, mellifluo, color pastello, qualcosa che in Occidente sarebbe improponibile dopo l'età di sette-otto anni e che invece in Giappone vende ai ragazzi e soprattutto alle ragazze dai cinque anni fino all'età del matrimonio" (p. 71). Del resto, dopo Murakami e il movimento Superflat ha ancora senso distinguere il gadget dall'opera d'arte?

Così lontane, così vicine. Come Pokémon e Tamagotchi, la mascotte è un catalizzatore di comportamenti di affezione. Gli appassionati delle mascotte finiscono per costituire delle tribù che trasformano l'oggetto-immagine in un comportamento collettivo isterico e rituale. Le mascotte sono un artefatto culturale, ma anche un fenomeno culturale. Si collocano al crocevia dei processi di contaminazione tra cultura occidentale e cultura orientale. Sono delle figure bizzarre eppure familiari. Il loro linguaggio visuale è tranquillizzante eppure arcano. Lungi dall'essere frequentate da una nicchia di cultori, le mascotte prevedono una dimensione di fruizione estesa e allargata. La mascotte occupa lo spazio ed il tempo: penso al calendario "kawaii" di Meomi Design, ma anche alle opere di Genevieve Gauckler, i cui pupazzi non solo hanno ridisegnato le figure dello zodiaco (vedi anche Yoko D'Holbachie), ma hanno ridisegnato gli spazi urbani e suburbani. E lo stesso vale per i graffiti surreali di Boris Hoppek. La mascotte non appartiene all'immaginario *fantasy*: a differenza dei folletti e degli gnomi, non vive in spazi marginali o alternativi, ma sembra trovarsi a suo agio tanto "nel mondo" quanto nel liquido amniotico del virtuale (non a caso, un *leit-motiv* di questa raccolta sono le figure ittiche e tentacolari, le pinne, le squame).

Concludiamo con una battuta che è anche una provocazione: se Frankenstein è figlio della rivoluzione industriale – è noto che l'ispirazione per la creazione del suo romanzo è venuta a Mary Shelley dopo aver visitato la collezione di automi del collezionista svizzero Jaquet-Droz – le mascotte sono il prodotto ultimo della rivoluzione digitale.

Morale della favola: **resistere è futile**.

MATTEO BITTANTI è uno studioso dei media che si interessa in particolare dell'intersezione tra arte, tecnologia e cultura pop. La sua ricerca è orientata sulle implicazioni culturali, sociali e teoriche delle tecnologie emergenti, con un'enfasi particolare sulle interrelazioni tra la cultura pop, la cultura visuale e l'arte. È l'autore di vari libri e saggi sui videogiochi, il cinema e la cultura del consumo. Il suo sito personale è Mattscape (www.mattscape.com). E-mail: mbittanti@libero.it

RIFERIMENTI BIBLIOGRAFICI

Carriker, K. (1998), *The Miniature Body of the Doll as Subject and Object*, Lehigh University Press, Londra.

Gerbert, E. (2001) "Dolls in Japan", *The Journal of Popular Culture*, Vol. 35.

Gomarasca, A. (2001) *La bambola e il robottone. Culture pop nel Giappone contemporaneo*. Einaudi, Torino.

Gomarasca & Valtorta (1996) *Sol mutante. Mode, giovani e umori nel Giappone contemporaneo*. Costa & Nolan, Genova,

Homes, A.H. (1991) *The safety of objects*, Vintage Books, New York (trad.it *La sicurezza degli oggetti*, minimum fax, Roma 2001).

King, S. (1985) *Skeleton Crew*, Putnam, New York (trad. it, *Scheletri*, Sperling & Kupfer, Milano, 1999).

McLuhan, M. (1964) *Understanding Media. The Extensions of Man*. Signet Classics, New York (trad. it. *Gli strumenti del comunicare*, Il Saggiatore, Milano, 1998).

Sconce, J. (2000) *Haunted Media: Electronic Presence from Telegraphy to Television*, Duke University Press, Durham.

Tanizaki, J. (1928) *Tade kuu mushi* (trad. it., *Gli insetti preferiscono le ortiche*, Mondadori, Milano 1960).

Meomi Design / *meomimessage*

graffiti... The mascot does not belong to the tradition of the *fantasy*: they are not elves or hobbits. They do not leave in parallel, alternative or marginal worlds. Rather, they share our own dimensions, the real and the amniotic liquid of the virtual (hence the leitmotiv of the fish-mascot). As Gergert (2001) suggests, "Such a belief in the power of the doll to transport love and good fortune may underlie the traditional Japanese custom of women taking along their ceremonial dolls when they left their natal homes to travel to the unfamiliar territory of their new homes" (p. 56). The mascots now accompany us in out virtual journeys.

A conclusion, a provocation: If Frankenstein is the outcome of the Industrial Revolution, created at the beginning of the machine age after Mary Shelley had seen a Swiss collection of remarkable androids owned by Jaquet-Droz, the mascot is the final outcome of the digital age.

Bottom line: resistance is futile.

MATTEO BITTANTI is a media practitioner/theorist who investigates the intersection of art, technology, and popular culture through critical writing. His research focuses on the cultural, social and theoretical aspects of emerging technology, with an emphasis on the interrelations of popular culture, visual culture and the arts. He is the author of several books and essays on videogames, cinema and consumerist culture. His personal website is Mattscape (www.mattscape.com). E-mail: mbittanti@libero.it

REFERENCES

Carriker, K. (1998), *The Miniature Body of the Doll as Subject and Object*, Lehigh University Press, Londra.

Gerbert, E. (2001) "Dolls in Japan", *The Journal of Popular Culture*, Vol. 35.

Gomarasca, A. (2001) *La bambola e il robottone. Culture pop nel Giappone contemporaneo*. Einaudi, Torino.

Gomarasca & Valtorta (1996) *Sol mutante. Mode, giovani e umori nel Giappone contemporaneo*. Costa & Nolan, Genova,

Homes, A.H. (1991) *The safety of objects*, Vintage Books, New York.

King, S. (1985) *Skeleton Crew*, Putnam, New York.

McLuhan, M. (1964) *Understanding Media. The Extensions of Man*. Signet Classics, New York

Sconce, J. (2000) *Haunted Media: Electronic Presence from Telegraphy to Television*, Duke University Press, Durham.

Tanizaki, J. (1928) *Tade kuu mushi*, Kodansha, Tokyo (*Some prefer nettles*, Vintage Books, October, New Yok, 1995).

12 geneviève gauckler Random Monster

GENEVIÈVE
GAUCKLER

france

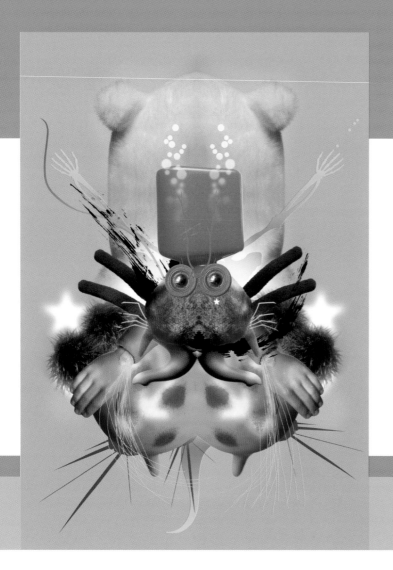

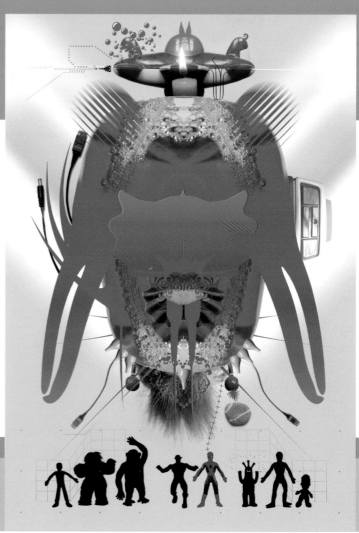

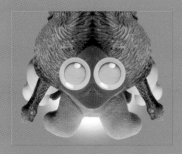

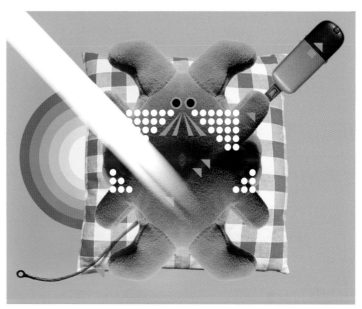

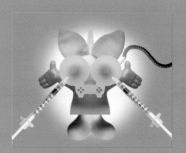

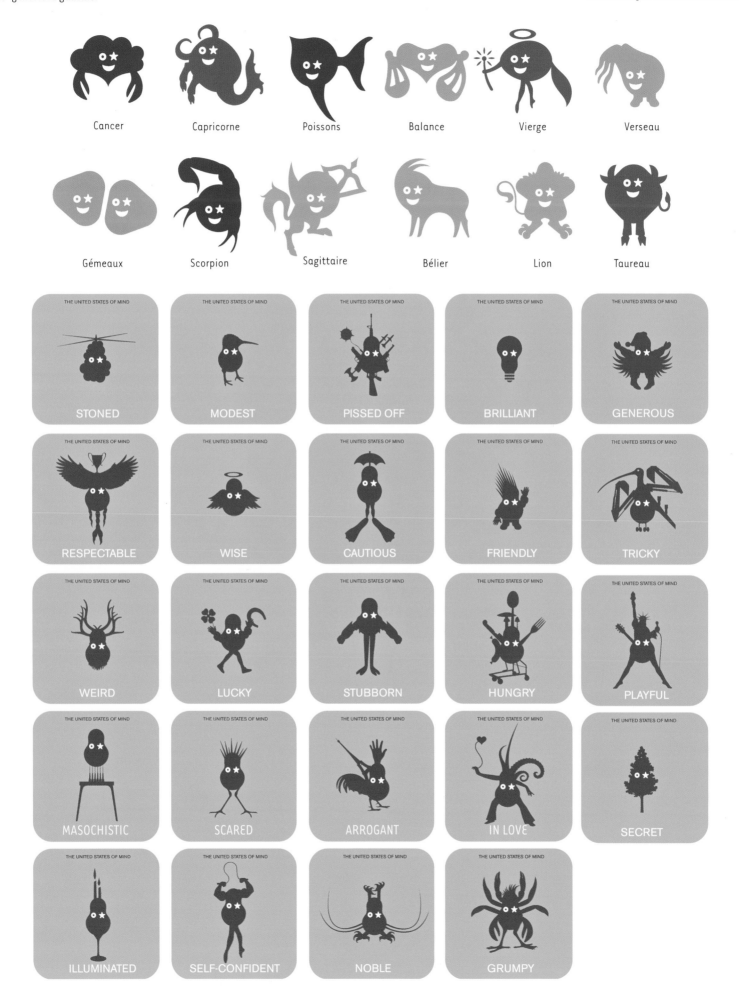

Cancer   Capricorne   Poissons   Balance   Vierge   Verseau

Gémeaux   Scorpion   Sagittaire   Bélier   Lion   Taureau

THE UNITED STATES OF MIND — STONED
THE UNITED STATES OF MIND — MODEST
THE UNITED STATES OF MIND — PISSED OFF
THE UNITED STATES OF MIND — BRILLIANT
THE UNITED STATES OF MIND — GENEROUS

THE UNITED STATES OF MIND — RESPECTABLE
THE UNITED STATES OF MIND — WISE
THE UNITED STATES OF MIND — CAUTIOUS
THE UNITED STATES OF MIND — FRIENDLY
THE UNITED STATES OF MIND — TRICKY

THE UNITED STATES OF MIND — WEIRD
THE UNITED STATES OF MIND — LUCKY
THE UNITED STATES OF MIND — STUBBORN
THE UNITED STATES OF MIND — HUNGRY
THE UNITED STATES OF MIND — PLAYFUL

THE UNITED STATES OF MIND — MASOCHISTIC
THE UNITED STATES OF MIND — SCARED
THE UNITED STATES OF MIND — ARROGANT
THE UNITED STATES OF MIND — IN LOVE
THE UNITED STATES OF MIND — SECRET

THE UNITED STATES OF MIND — ILLUMINATED
THE UNITED STATES OF MIND — SELF-CONFIDENT
THE UNITED STATES OF MIND — NOBLE
THE UNITED STATES OF MIND — GRUMPY

Elastic guys

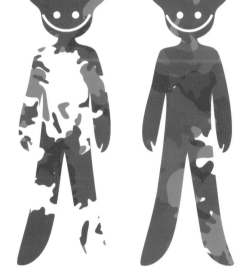

Ninja guys

Camo guys

Rounded guys

Northern brothers

Peace guy

Northern brothers

Aj!

Logo boo.com

being happy.

planting a tree.

visiting a new city and getting lost.

meditating.

demonstrating.

Geneviève Gauckler

L'arbre génialogique

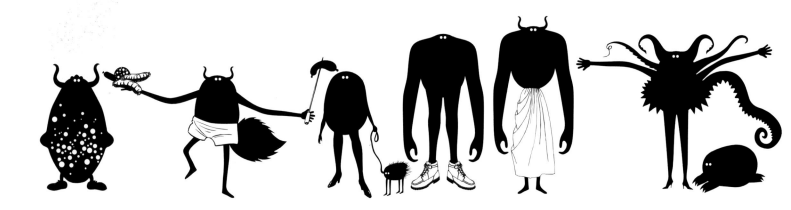

15

Quel choc pour Louise. Une vision de cauchemar s'empara d'elle.

23

Le plus difficile à vivre était finalement le regard des autres.

32

Il sentait bien que tout le monde le regardait.

33

MEOMi DESiGN

canada

十一月｜november 2002

S	M	T	W	T	F	S
					1	2
3	4	5	6	7	8	9
10	11	12	13	14	15	16
17	18	19	20	21	22	23
24	25	26	27	28	29	30

四月｜april 2002

S	M	T	W	T	F	S
	1	2	3	4	5	6
7	8	9	10	11	12	13
14	15	16	17	18	19	20

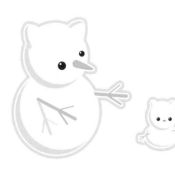

一月 | JANUARY 2002

S	M	T	W	T	F	S
		1	2	3	4	5
6	7	8	9	10	11	12
13	14	15	16	17	18	19
20	21	22	23	24	25	26
27	28	29	30	31		

六月 | JUNE 2002

S	M	T	W	T	F	S
						1
2	3	4	5	6	7	8
9	10	11	12	13	14	15
16	17	18	19	20	21	22
23	24	25	26	27	28	29
30						

fly away
meomi

ABOVE: Fil d'Ariane *Logo branding, illustration for brochure, stickers and t-shirts.*
MIDDLE: Meomi Sticker *inhouse promotion*
BELOW: Snowday, *Zinc Roe - interactive flash video*

SHOPPING

GOURMAND

PRATIQUE

SPORT ET LOISIR

NUIT

ART ET CULTURE

BEAUTE

LE FIL D'ARIANE

the SHAKE

the SHAKE

the Shake

the Shake

Tipper, CBC4Kids (Canadian Broadcasting Corporation) www.cbc4kids.com, Interactive storybuilder

JEAN-MARIE ANGLES
france

"My characters are made with PLASTIBO (a synthetic material who becomes hard with the air) shaped on a wire frame work. The settings are made with different materials according to the atmosphere I want to give".

JEAN-MARIE ANGLES

ABOVE: detail / BELOW: les peintres + le déménageur / france telecom / agence metzler & associés / photographer: fabrice besse/studio cactus

ABOVE: detail / BELOW: la musicienne / france telecom / agence metzler & associés / photographer: fabrice besse/studio cactus

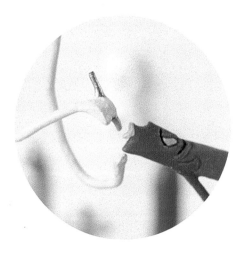

ABOVE:le cracheur de feu + la vendeuse de légumes / france telecom / agence metzler & associés / photographer: fabrice besse/studio cactus / BELOW: la chinoise - photographer: pascal legrand

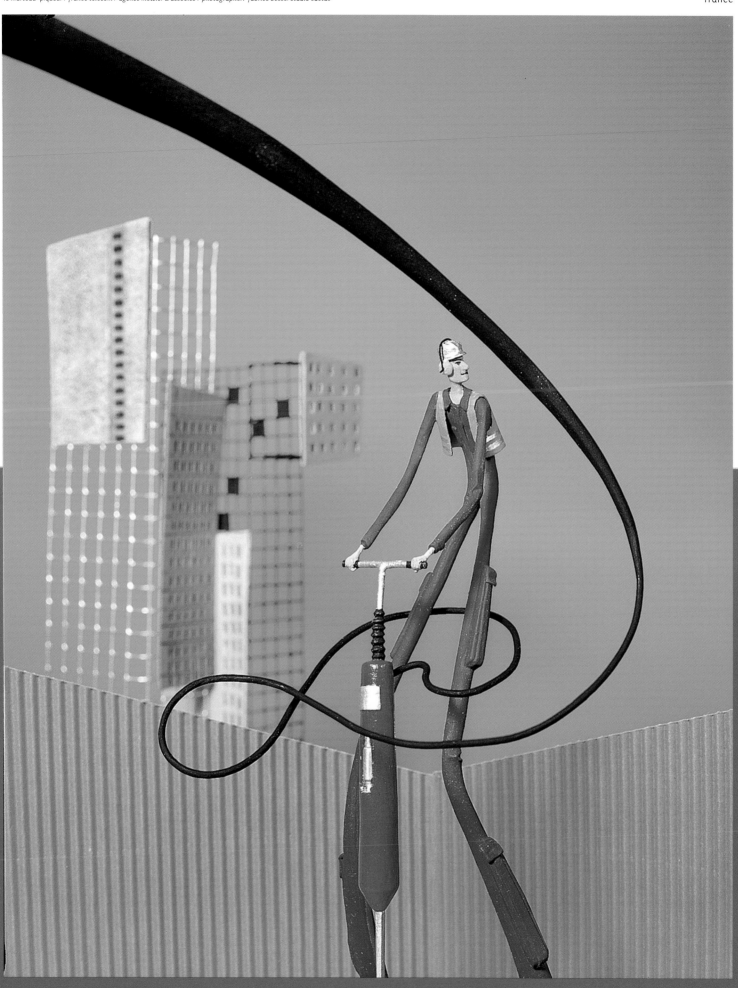

42 doudouboy

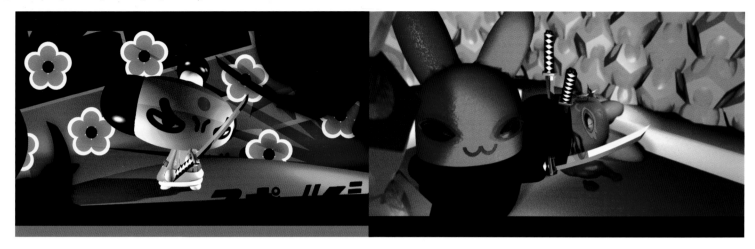

DOUDOUBOY
france

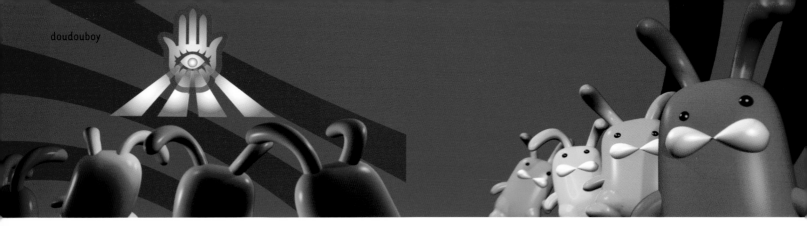

doudouboy

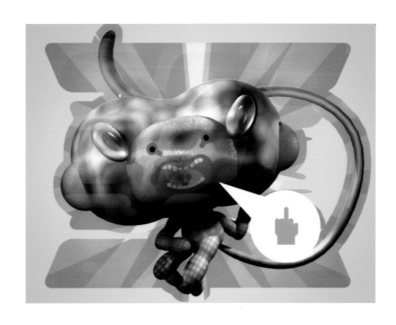

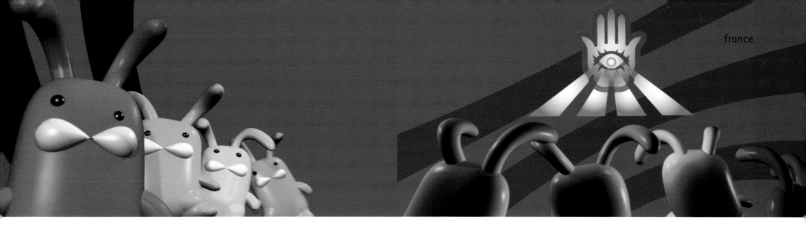

TINMYL
COMP. 1

KEN HOSHINO
japan

aep
animal electrical products

*This is a plan page of an imaginary company,
"animal electrical products" on purpose of
display and presentation.
All these 3D illustrations are based on an idea of
"how exciting if there would be..."*

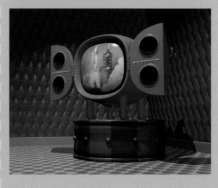

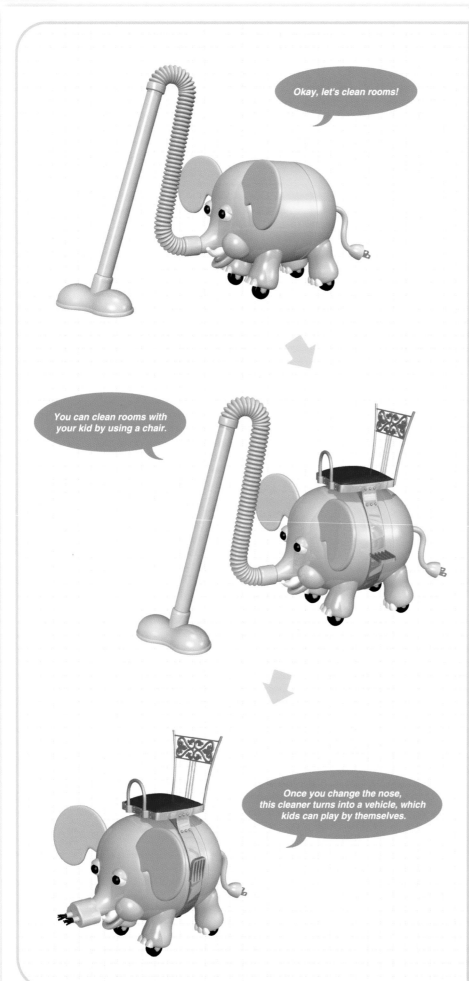

Super hanage broom
Please attach this broom to the nose when you clean narrow places.
* "Hanage" means the hairs in the nostrils.

Feet steps
Please open the steps and put your kid's feet on the steps when you use this vacuum, riding your kid.

Tail plug
The tail is an elastic plug.

aep
animal electrical products
http://www.tcp-ip.or.jp/~kenken/

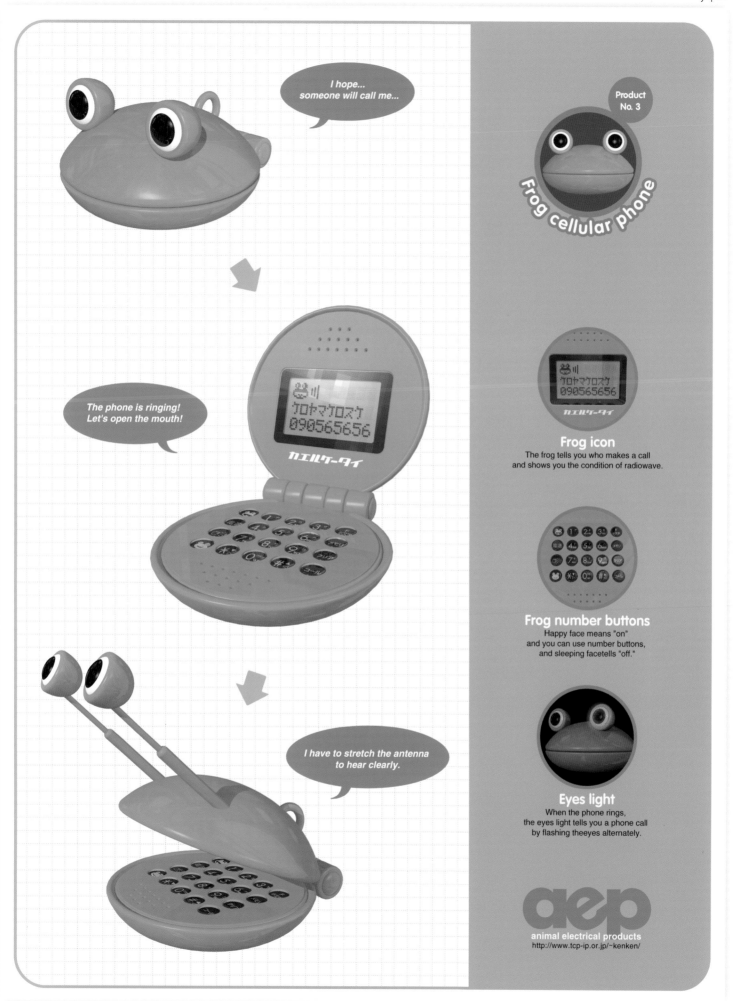

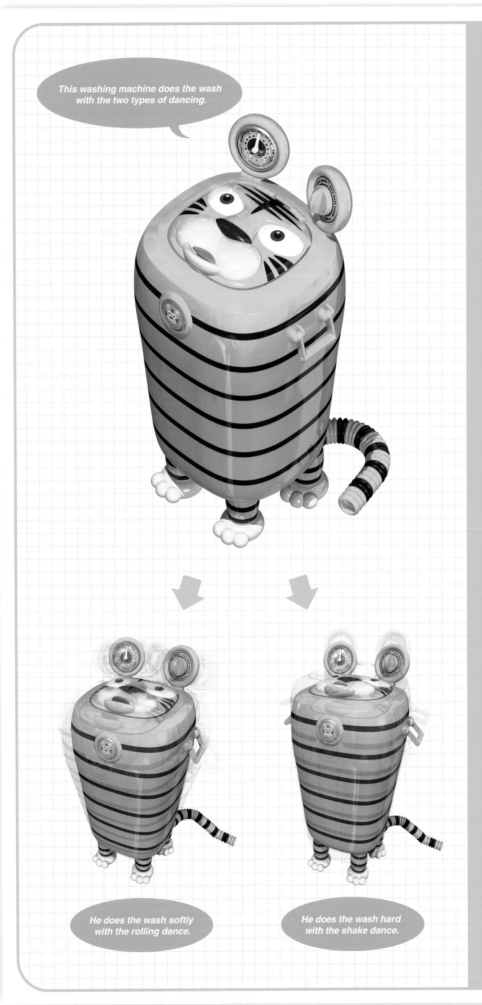

This washing machine does the wash with the two types of dancing.

He does the wash softly with the rolling dance.

He does the wash hard with the shake dance.

Product No. 4

Tiger washing machine

Ear meter
The right ear is the meter panel which shows washing condition.

Tiger turning drum
When you open the tiger face, it's a turning drum and the color is red.

Tail hose
The tail is elastic and alterable, and it's a drain hose.

animal electrical products
http://www.tcp-ip.or.jp/~kenken/

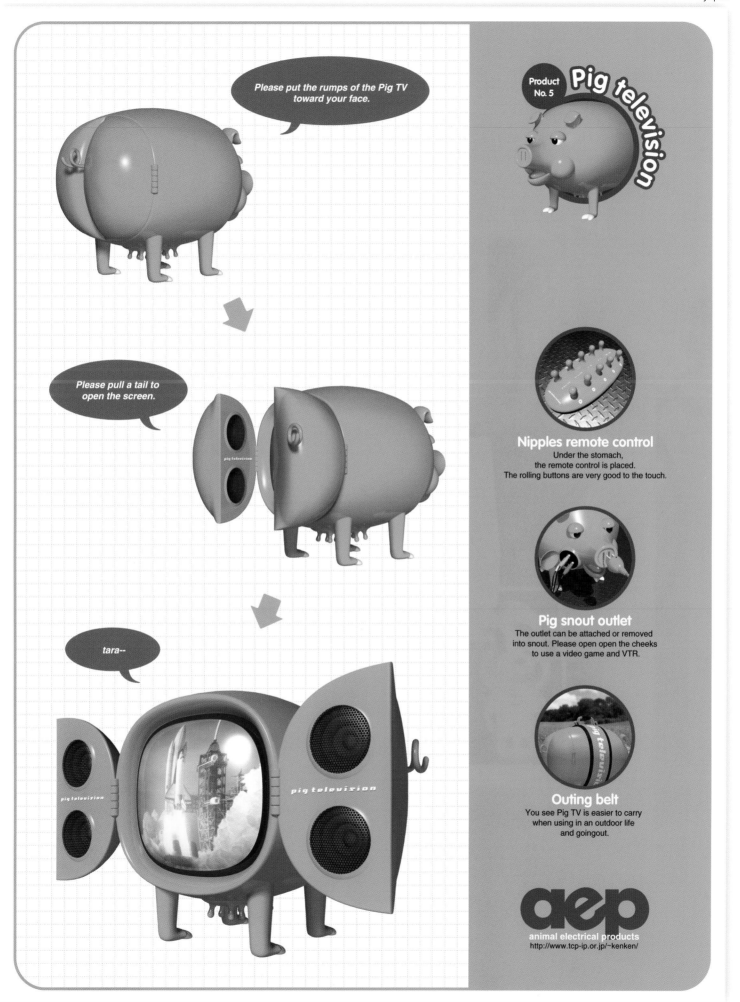

The story of Zizi and Jojo

jojo

tiger Jo

Zizi

There is a race held on 10 circuits, which consists of the 9 planets in the Galaxy and the moon. Everyone competes for an annual champion.

This is the highest Galaxy race- Galaxy One [G1].
In the [G1], one racing team has done wonders, that is, Rabbit racing team won 9 consecutive champs. The ace drivers of the team are legendary twins- zizi and jojo. Zizi and jojo were born in the poorest star, the moon; however, they yearned for G1 racer, seeing a moon racing when young, and it brought them to a racer.
With innate ability and effort, zizi and jojo stood out as a racer. Before long, they were scouted for Rabbit racing team, then theyachieved 9 consecutive champs.
At that time, a special machine of Rabbit racing helped the 9 champs.

This machine is equipped with two jet engines, succeeds in lightening its weight without limit, and responds to handling promptly. Therefore, the 9 consecutive champs were accomplished by the trust of drivers in Rabbit racing. Zizi, jojo, and Rabbit racing are passed from mouth to mouth as the greatest hero in the moon.

Then, tiger Jo is the closest rival to Zizi and Jojo.
Using a high-powered machine, which is equipped with three jet enjines, he has won the champ in Galaxy One [G1] many times. However, the remarkable achivement of Zizi and Jojo put him into the shade.

So, he drills his son, tiger Jo Jr., in a special training and plans to get back the glory again.

PACO AGUAYO
mexico

ciertas ideas
se gestan en capullos...
anhelan volar

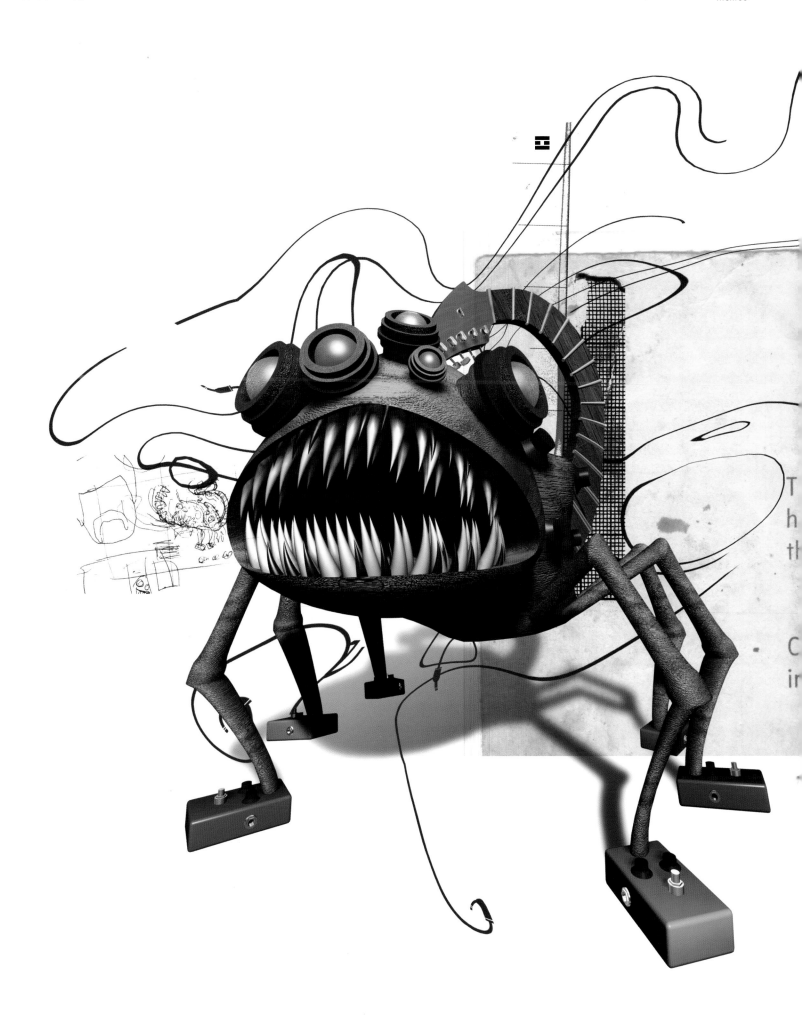

Señor
Cabezahueca

...sado de pensar, de cuestionar, de im...
...o vive para funcionar, como una pie...
...la máquina de consumo. Vive de la i...
...el aparador, no conoce la emoción, s...
...ción. Ahorro. Cálculo renal. Inversi...
...guro de vida. No le gusta soñar. No...
...rar el cielo. El último banquete de lo...
...los. Un maletín lleno de papeles. Un...
...razón de piedra. Un aspecto simpátic...
...o. Ayudame! (dice por dentro) pero n...
...presa. El tiempo corre más rápido de...
...puedes correr. Te va a tocar al homb...
...onreir. Recordaras tu vida en un seg...
...spues?. El frio. Tu mirada vacia. Nad...

sin agua no hay vida
campaña para el cuidado del agua

sin agua no hay vida
campaña para el cuidado del agua

Polaroids del pasado

Por haber compartido una parte de tu vida conmigo.
Por todos esos momentos felices, en los que la sencillez
nos abrazaba. Por todas y cada una de tus sonrisas.
Gracias Tania.

Mixed-Clients / Pujol-Communication / T.O.C Magazine / 10 fingers, 2 hands, fimo clay

LA PATAMODELEUSE

JOSEPHINE PUJOS

france

Luciole-Circus / Self-Promotion / 10 fingers, 2 hands, fimo clay, paper an

the world famous

LUCIOLE CIRCUS

THE GREAT COSTELLO

PERFORMING FOR YOUR PLEASURE FOR ONE NIGHT ONLY!
WWW.LAPATAMODELEUSE.COM

Twice Daily . 2 & 8 P.M.
DOORS OPEN   1 & 7 P.M.
Tickets now on sale

Popular Prices

BORIS HOPPEK

germany

bimbousa
one who is blond,
one who is a sex object
with syntetics

bimboitaly
one who is young and male,
one who is a boy

bimbogermany
one who is black, dirty, stupid, ugly, lazy . . .
one who is black and proud

bimbojapan
one who is poor,
one who has no money

bimbo wilder

kkk bimbo

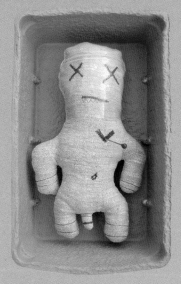

voodoo bimbo

wilder bimbo

stolen cushion wilder bimbo

bimbopussy

bimba bimbo

schweinehund bimbo

baby bimbo

hawaii bimbo

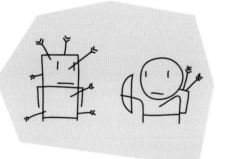

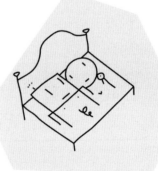

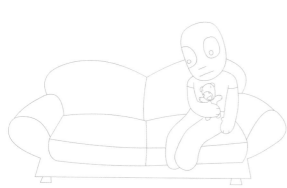

boris at urban-art.info
zeichnungen & skulpturen
19.juli - 18.august

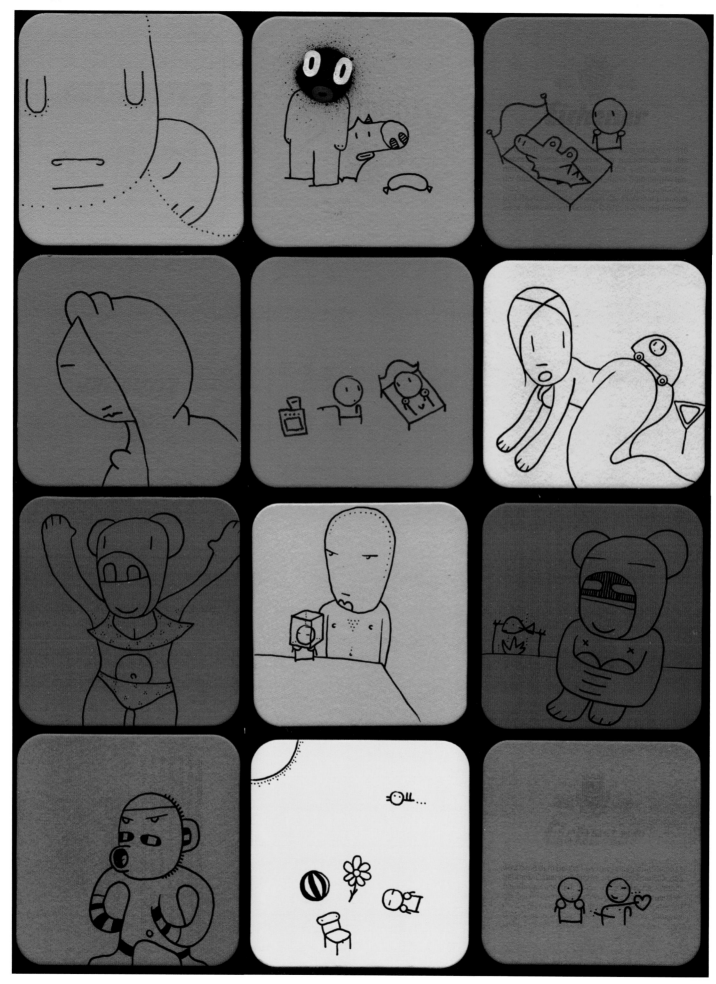

TINOLAND

france

zazou.gif
26,4 Ko
30/05/02

wattie.gif
52,5 Ko
30/05/02

voeux2003.jpg
399,9 Ko
27/01/03

vero.gif
38,4 Ko
30/05/02

toaster.gif
33,7 Ko
30/05/02

tino.gif
78,9 Ko
30/05/02

tati3.gif
49,0 Ko
30/05/02

tati2.gif
53,4 Ko
30/05/02

tati1.gif
31,1 Ko
30/05/02

somoeil.gif
6,2 Ko
30/05/02

schwendiland2.gif
33,7 Ko
30/05/02

piero2.gif
59,1 Ko
30/05/02

piero.gif
51,1 Ko
30/05/02

photo002anim.gif
17,7 Ko
30/05/02

petits_leoni.gif
66,7 Ko
4/10/02

louna.jpg
12,8 Ko
30/05/02

laurette2.gif
55,5 Ko
30/05/02

laurette.gif
46,3 Ko
30/05/02

jerome.gif
54,7 Ko
30/05/02

jeanne.gif
20,2 Ko
30/05/02

jc.gif
41,9 Ko
30/05/02

jan.gif
28,0 Ko
30/05/02

image10.gif
30,1 Ko
30/05/02

gilles.gif
71,8 Ko
4/12/02

gilbert.gif
72,8 Ko
4/12/02

gianni2.gif
38,4 Ko
30/05/02

gianni.gif
40,1 Ko
30/05/02

gaziniere1.gif
41,3 Ko
30/05/02

flore2.gif
44,4 Ko
30/05/02

flore.gif
36,0 Ko
30/05/02

famille.gif
62,8 Ko
30/05/02

eric.gif
53,8 Ko
30/05/02

emilie.gif
50,9 Ko
30/05/02

dume.gif
28,4 Ko
30/05/02

coucou.gif
40,4 Ko
30/05/02

claude4.gif
49,4 Ko
30/05/02

claude3.gif
34,2 Ko
30/05/02

claude2.gif
32,6 Ko
30/05/02

claude1.gif
36,3 Ko
30/05/02

brice.gif
27,0 Ko
30/05/02

laCAF avec vous
Allocations logement
...partout
Allocation aux adultes handicapés
la CAF avec vous
Soutien aux centres socioculturels
Allocation pour jeune enfant
CAF
Soutien aux équipements
Soutien aux collectivités

FORUM

cover for La Poste magazine [sccketches and print]

LA POSTE

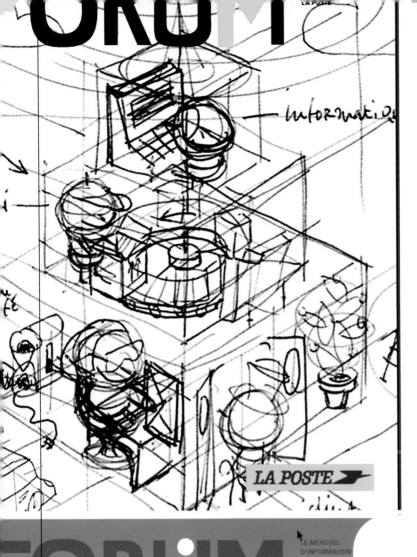

LE MENSUEL
D'INFORMATION
DU GROUPE
LA POSTE

FORUM

LE MENSUEL
D'INFORMATION
DU GROUPE
LA POSTE

LA POSTE

YUKIO KUWAJIMA

japan

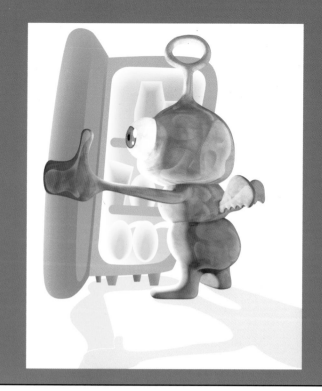

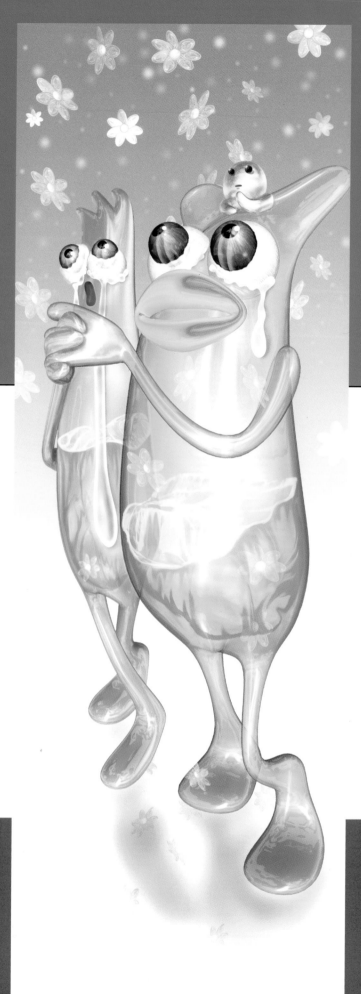

LEFT PAGE - above left: The fun of midnight/*Canon* above right: Oh!/*personal work* - below: It was wonderful to meet you/*personal work*
RIGHT PAGE: above left: I'm energetic!/*personal work* - above middle: The tired youngster/*personal work* - above right:Everybody loves Ramen/*personal work* - below: Heartbreak/*personal work*

japan   89

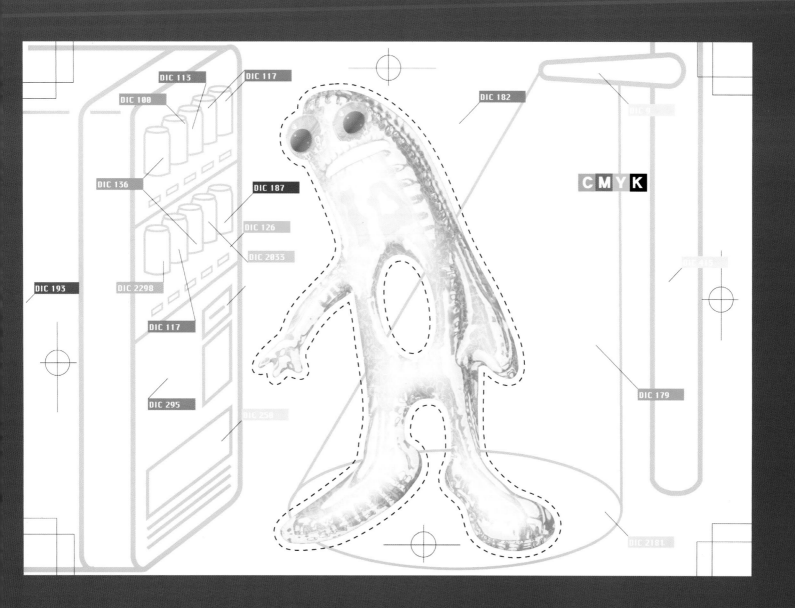

Above: after school hero
Below: Hey, there is a UFO!

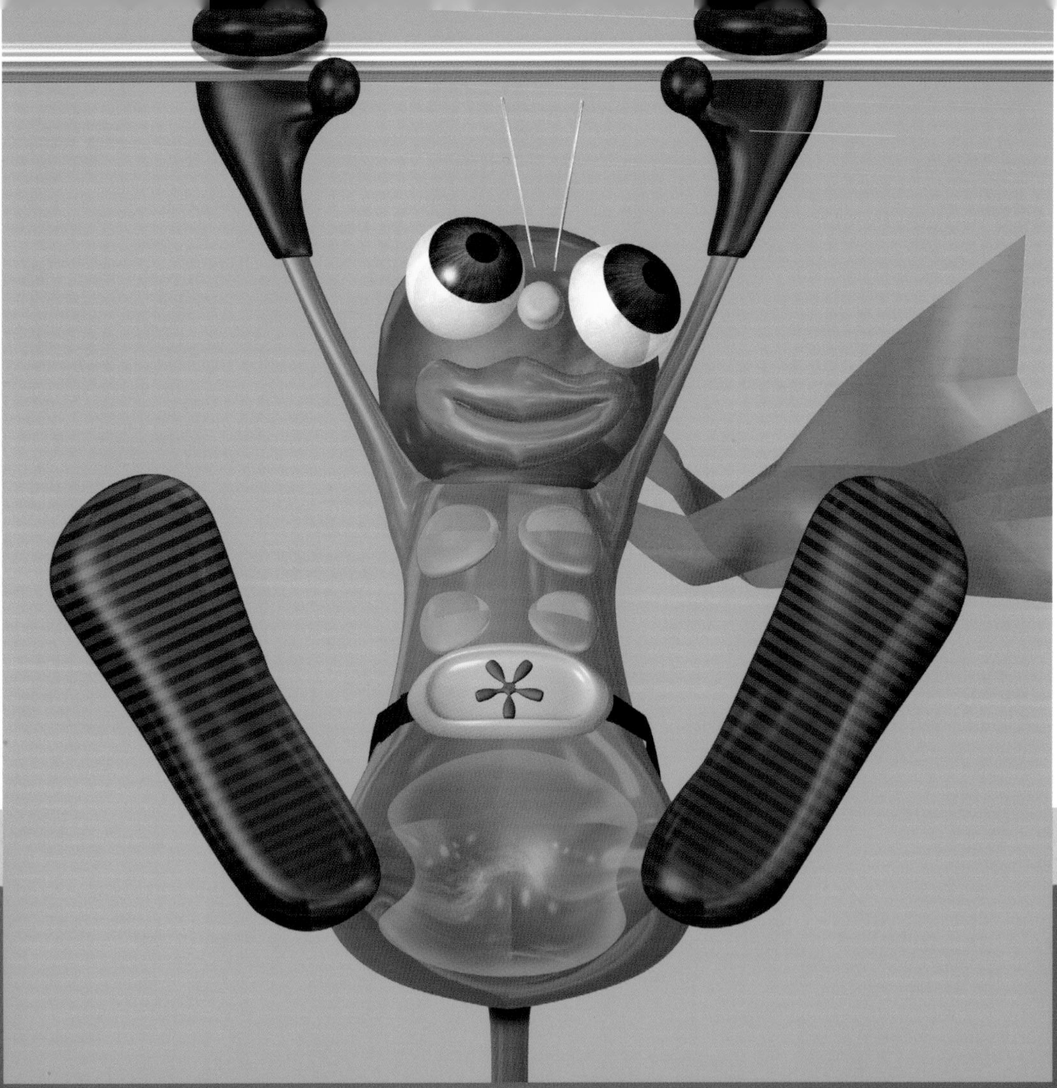

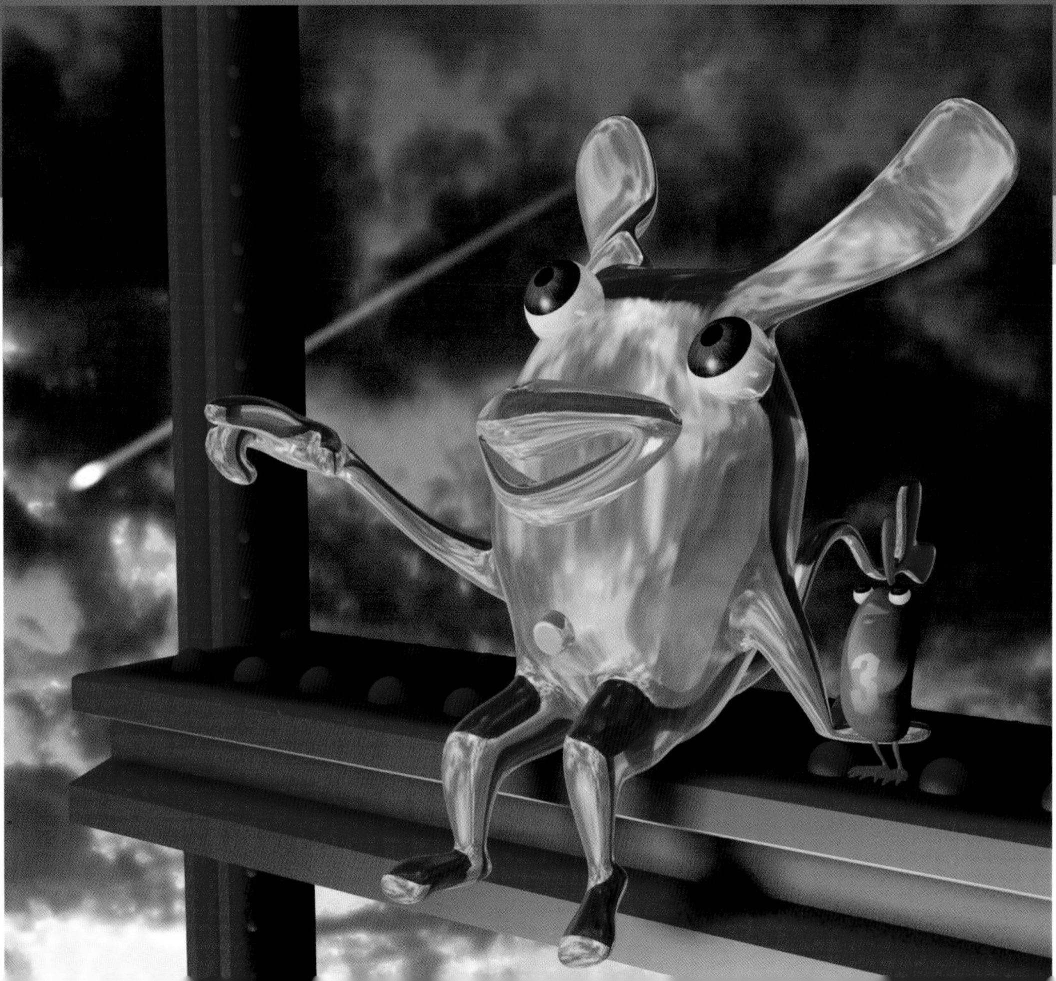

NATSUKO KOGURE

japan

Above left: angler / *personal work* – Below left: Scallop / *personal work* – Below right: the man of coral / *personal work*

japan   95

How to make papier-mache

1. Make a model from clay.

2. Stick a newspaper from on the.

3. Make it dry.

4. Take out inner clay.

5. A newspaper ties a crack and build a fine portion by hand.

6. Apply a white paint.

7. Color with acrylics paints.

Above left: japanese sea slug/*personal work* - Above right:sea anemone/ *personal work*
Below: small octopus/*personal work*

japan   97

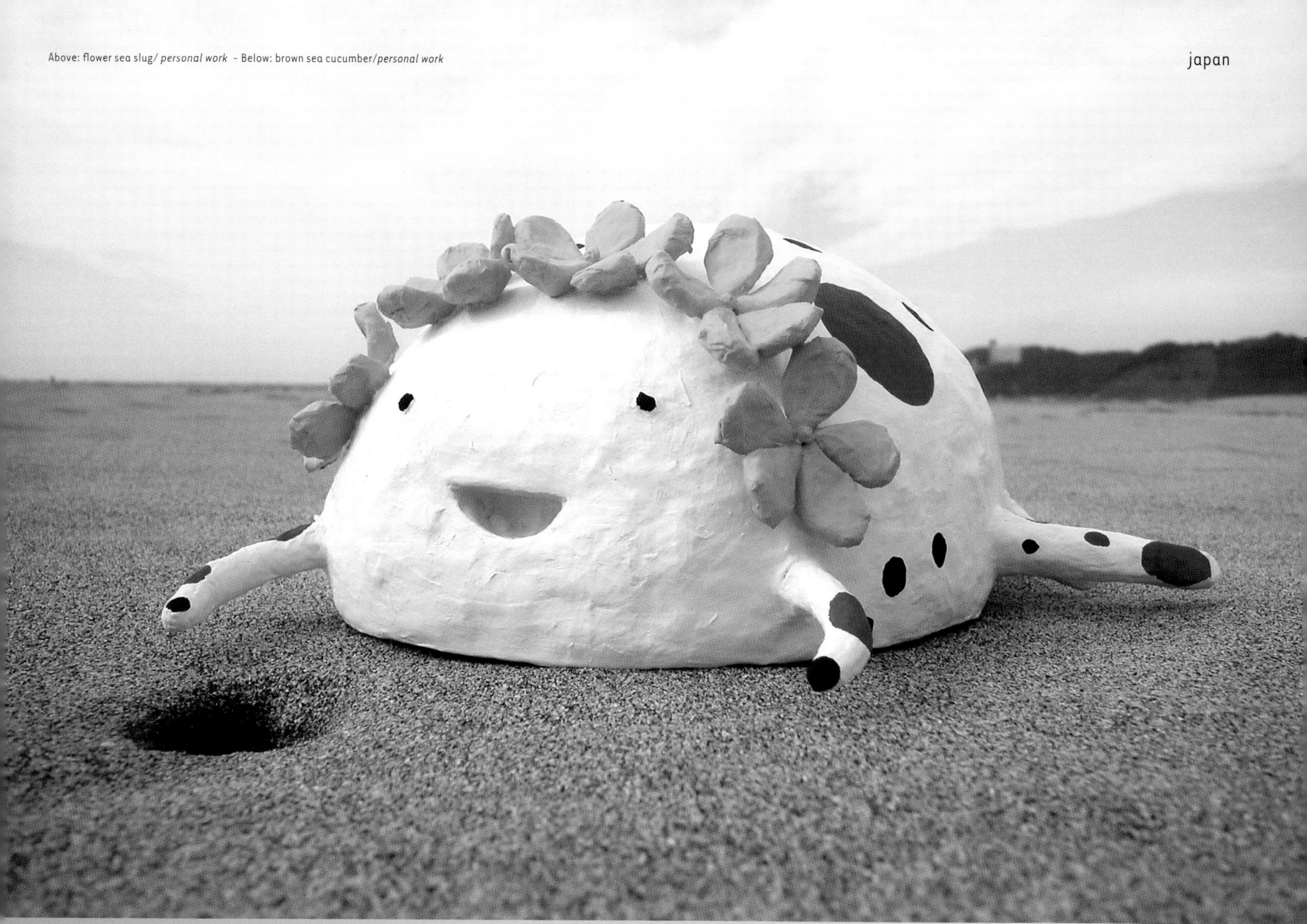

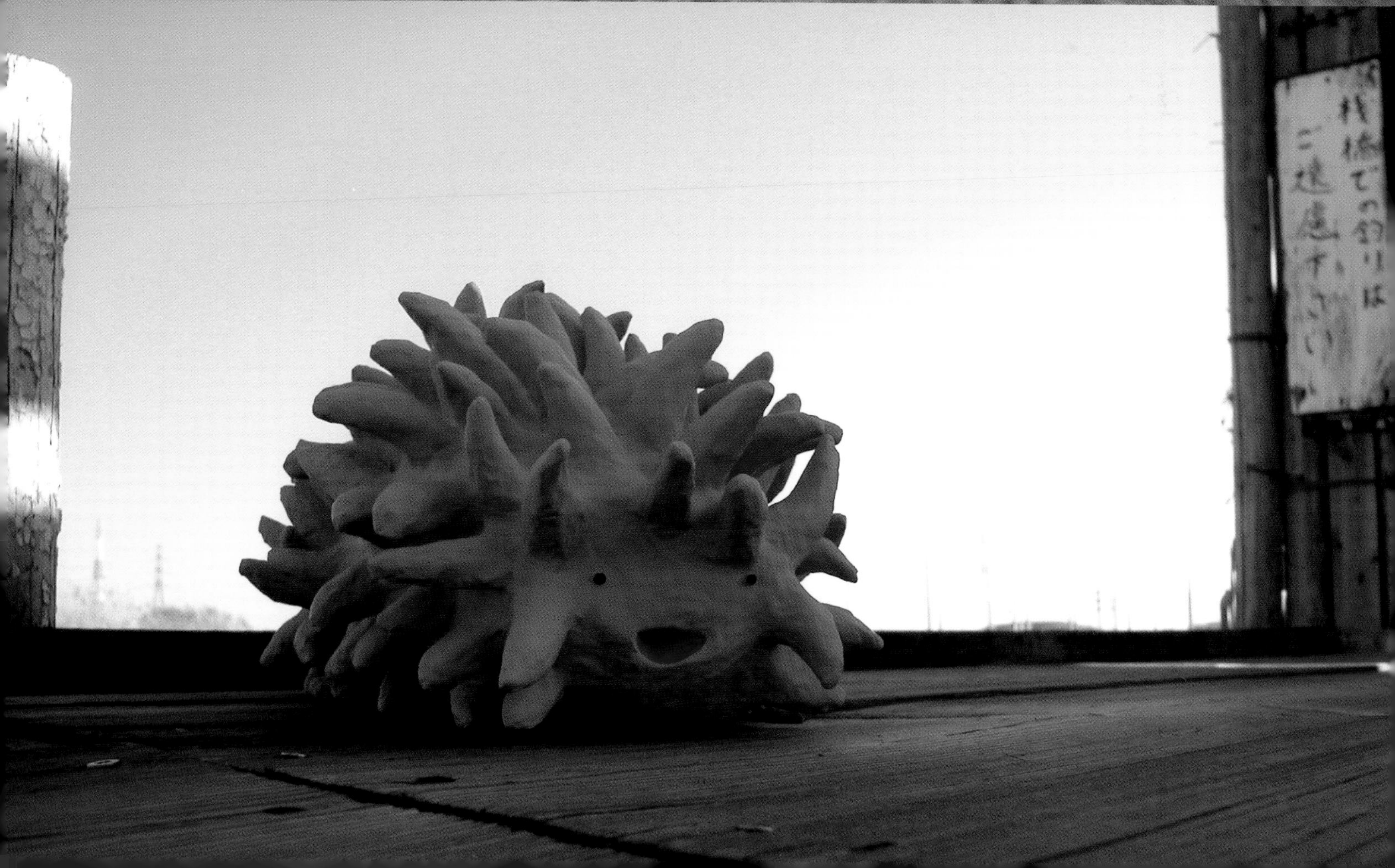
桟橋での釣りは
ご遠慮下さい

102 frederic pèault

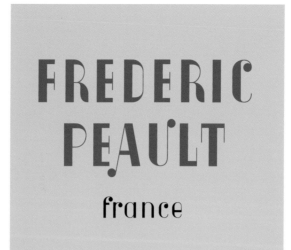

FREDERIC PEAULT

france

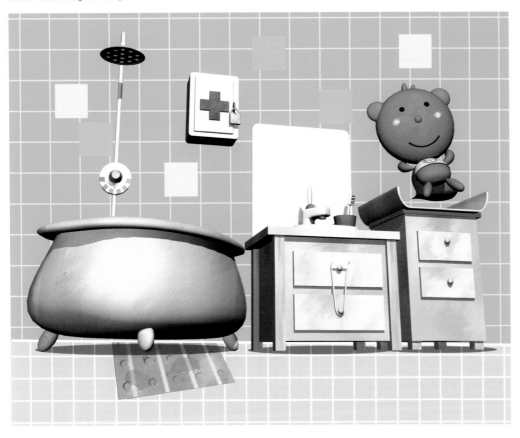

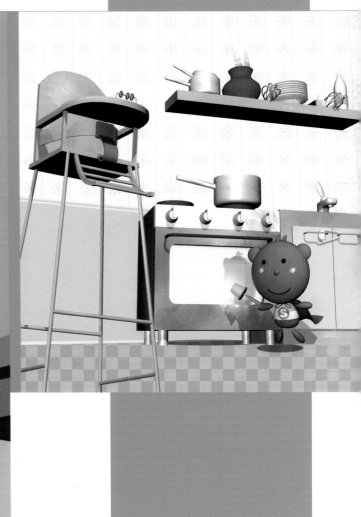

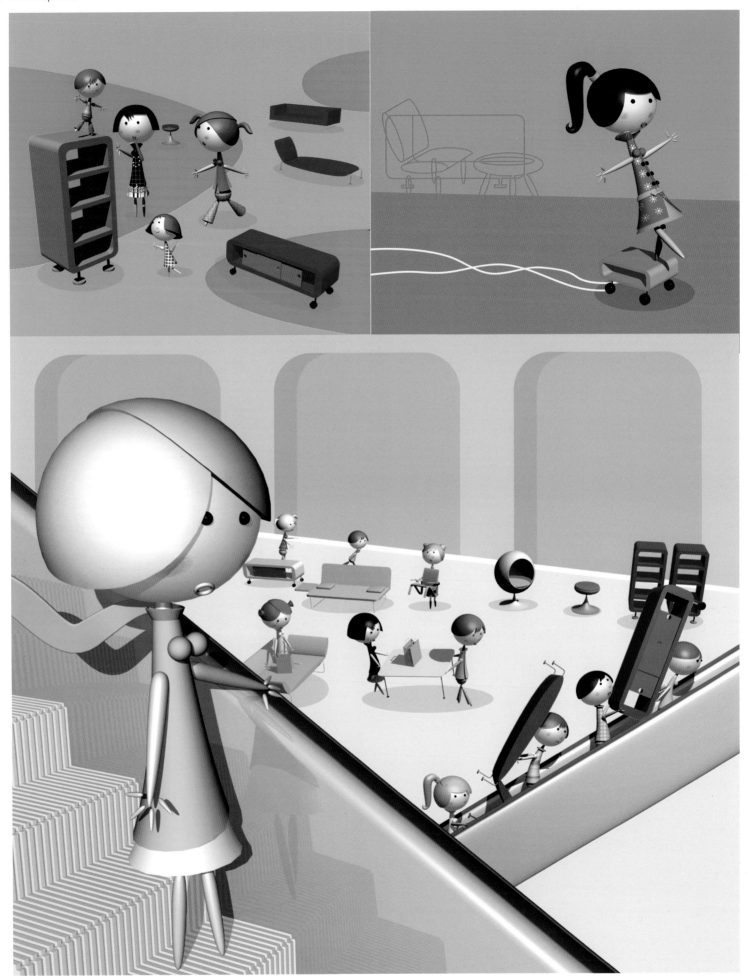

j'aime
beaucoup
mon fauteuil

NICOLA

japan

Above left: guardian dog/*personal work* - Above right: gooshang/*Fab communications co. ltd* - Below left: chief sonchou/*Fab communications co. ltd* - Below right: sharon/*Fab communications co. ltd*

KANAE ASAI

japan

Above left: bubble/*Okina* - Above right: petite fools/*personal work* - Below left: reading/*Okina* - Below left: cycling/*Okina*

japan 117

SATOMI YAI

japan

TART

COOKIE

BIRD

CANDY

CREAM

Mille-feuille

Live in the country

DOGGY

RABY

CYBER PETS

We are your pets that do to be happy.

CYBER PETS

We are your pets that do to be happy.

CATY

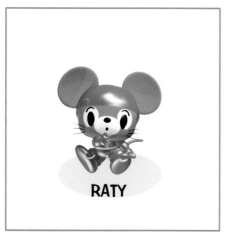

RATY

CYBER PETS

We are your pets that do to be happy.

PoLE PoLE

we are spirited puppys

Bee Attack

ONE DAY,
THEY ATTACKED
MANY BEES.
ROMP FIGHTED BRAVELY
AGAINST BEES.

BIB

ROMP

NAPPY

POLE PoLE

spirited puppys

THEY ARE ALWAYS
SPIRITED PUPPYS.
WHEN THEY ACT,
THEY CAUSE A TROUBLE.

BEE-BE-BROTHERS

D'HOLBACHIE YOKO

japan

Above: MILK MEN/illustration for PC magazine[MAC FAN] Copyright (C) MYCOM - Below: Three Jelly Fish/Animation for children Copyright(C) 2003 ALC

MUSHROOM*ROOM

CHILD
will be
CHILD

PEKAPOO PECANPIE (sleeping lotus)

HIROSHI YOSHII

japan

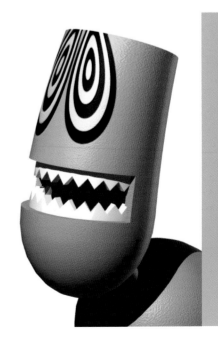

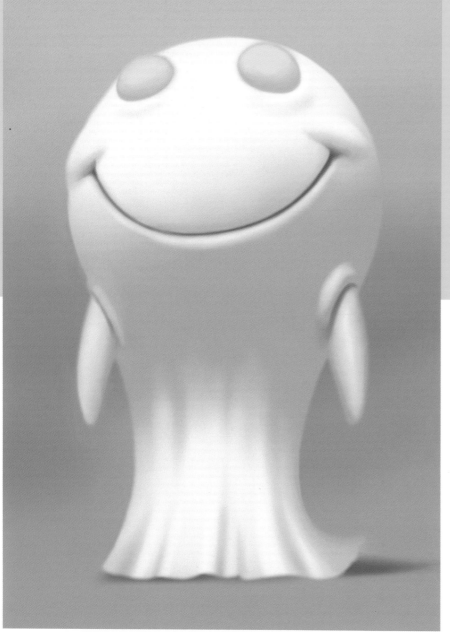

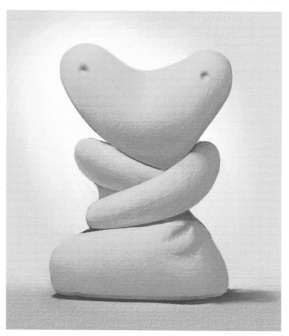

Baloon Cow

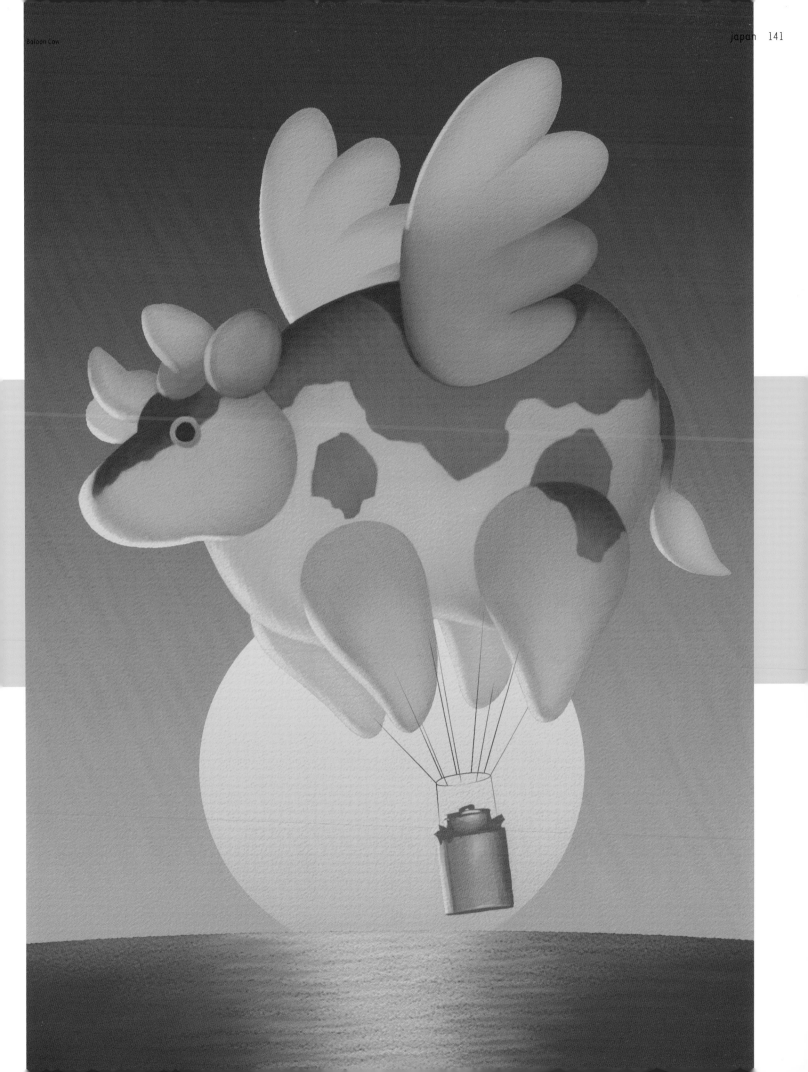

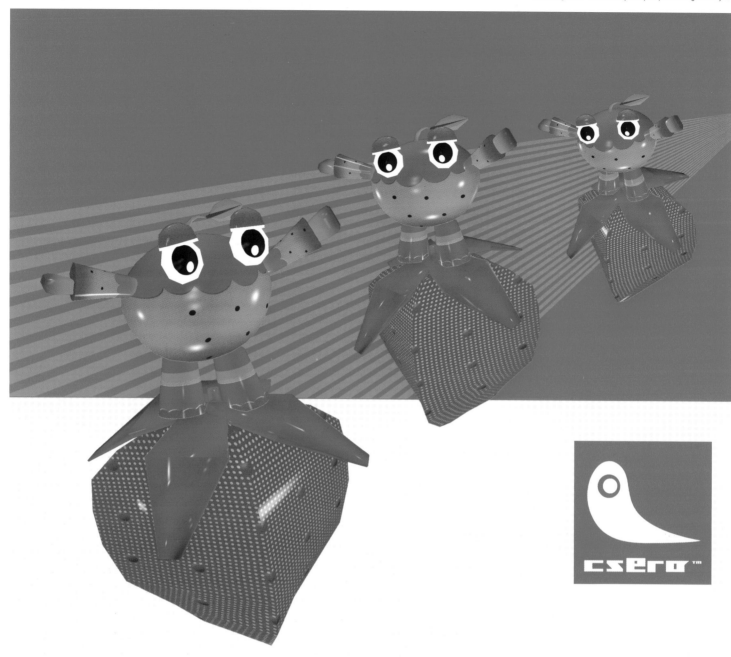

IAN STOKES

united states

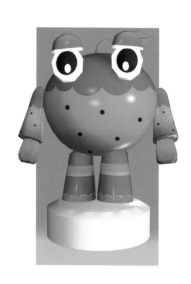

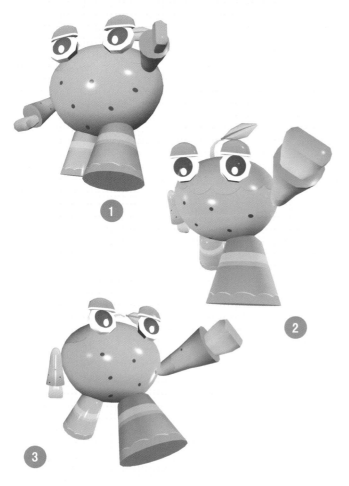

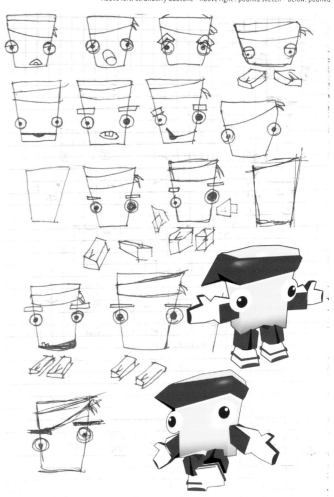

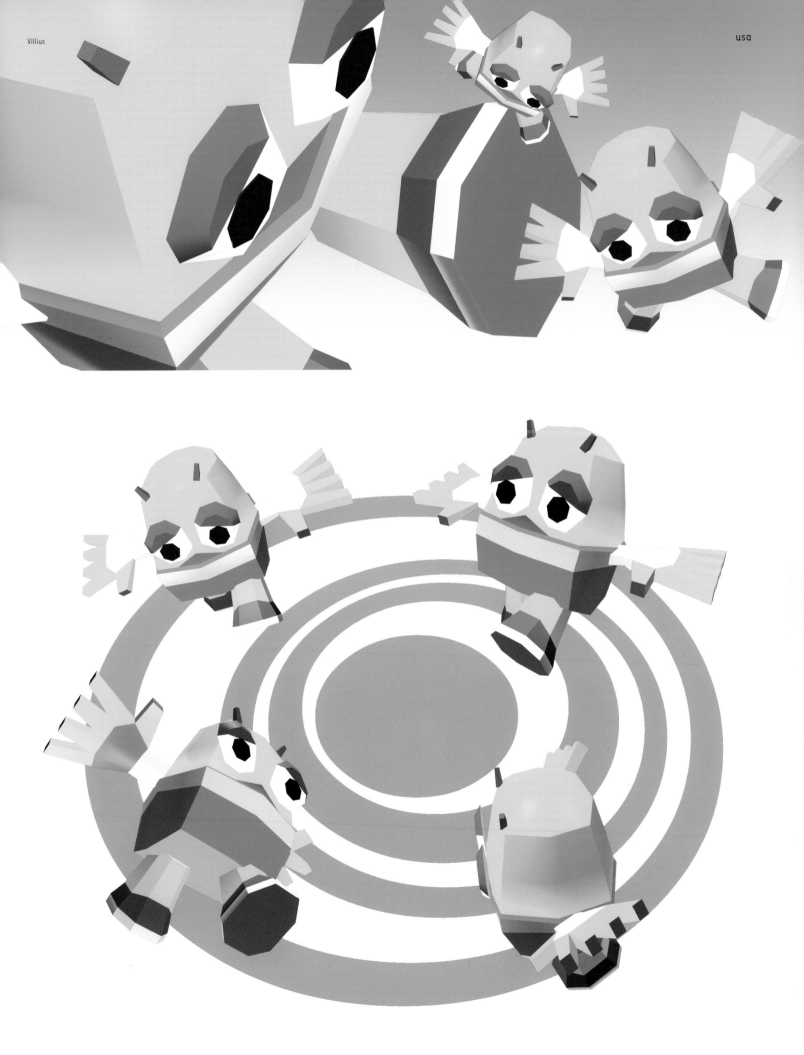

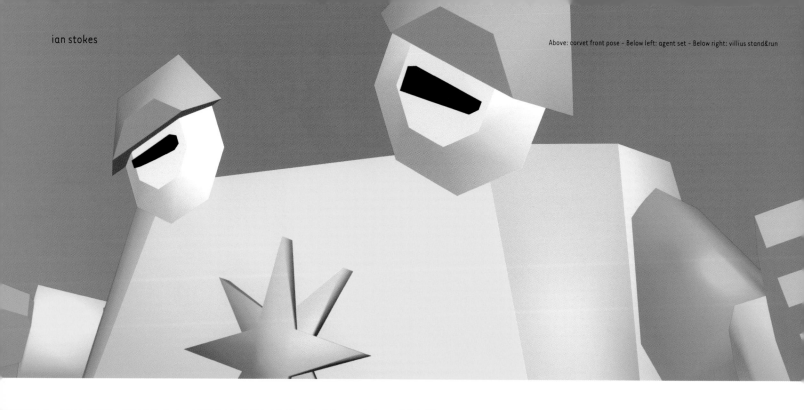

152 mamiko hasebe

MAMIKO HASEBE
japan

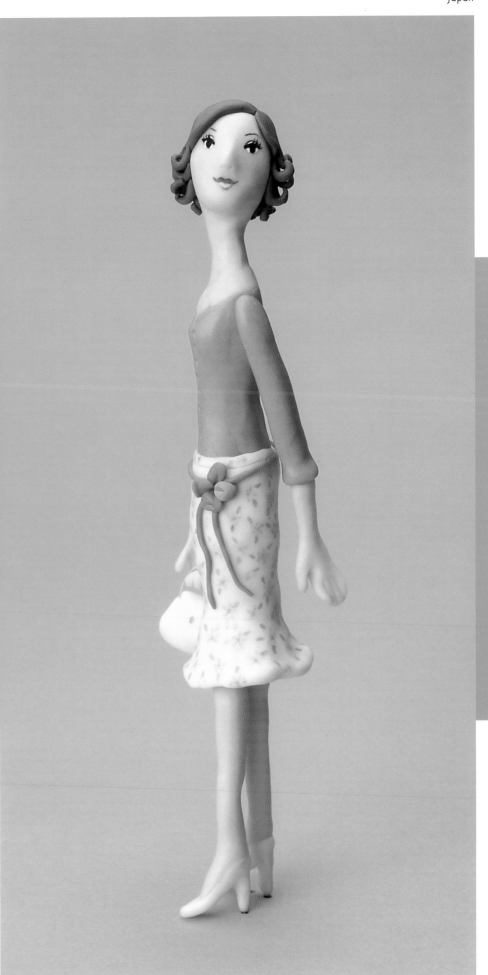

RAFAEL MENDOZA

mexico

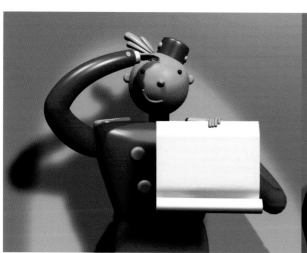

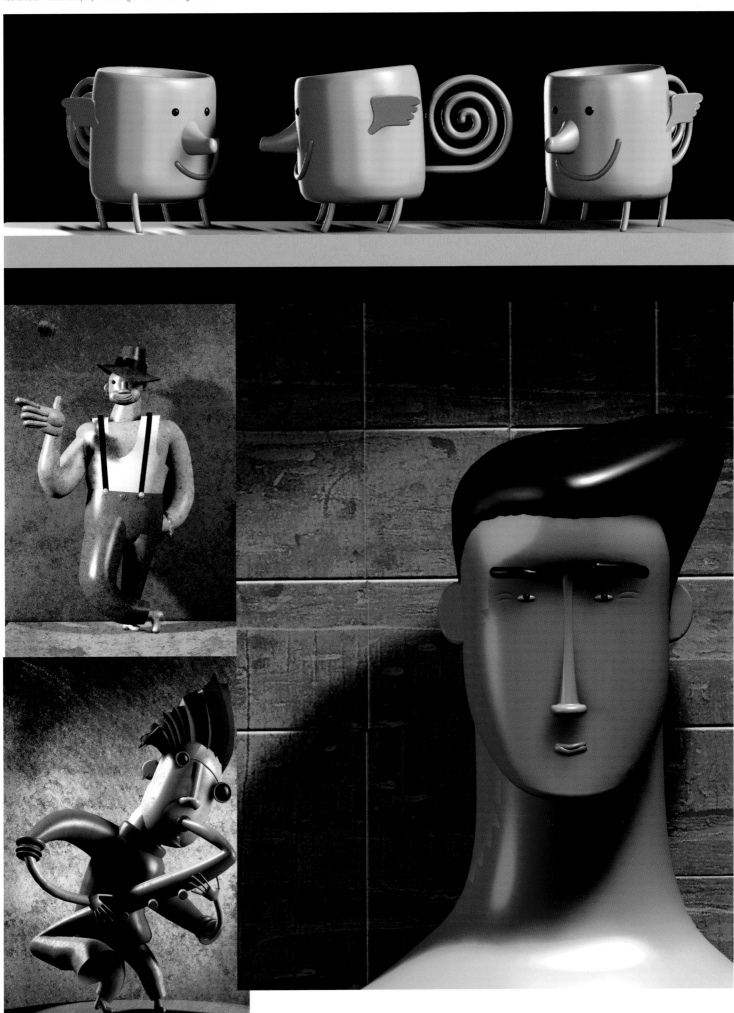

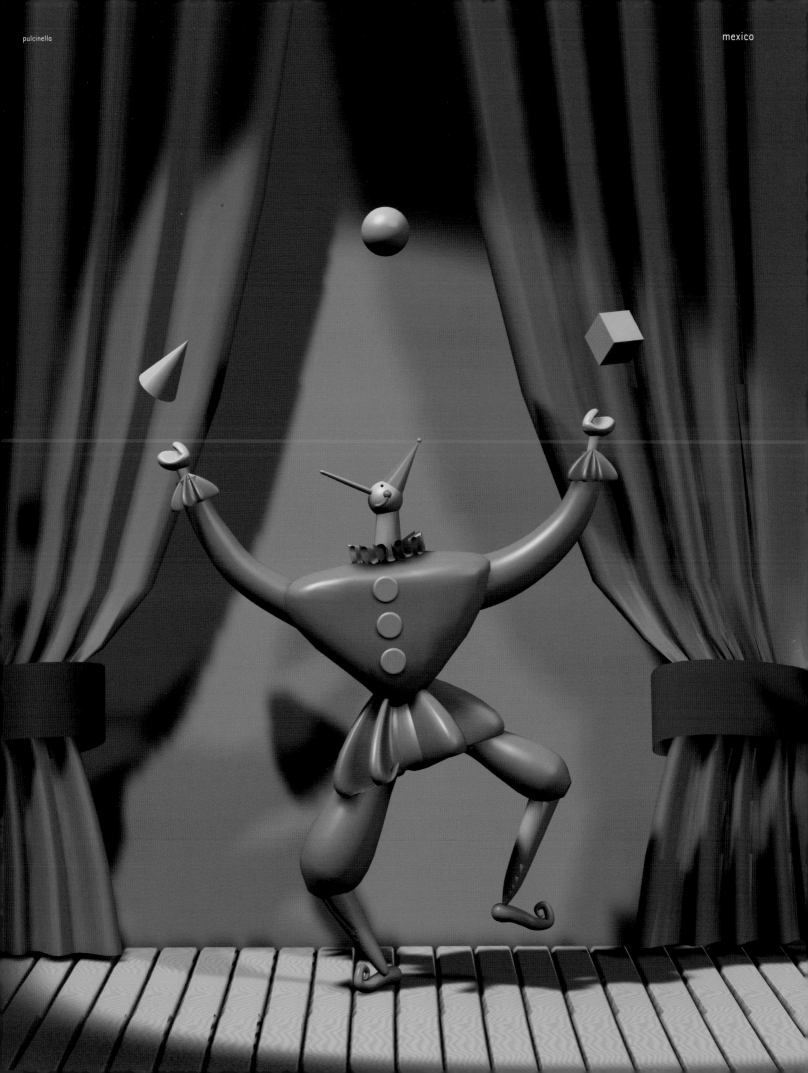

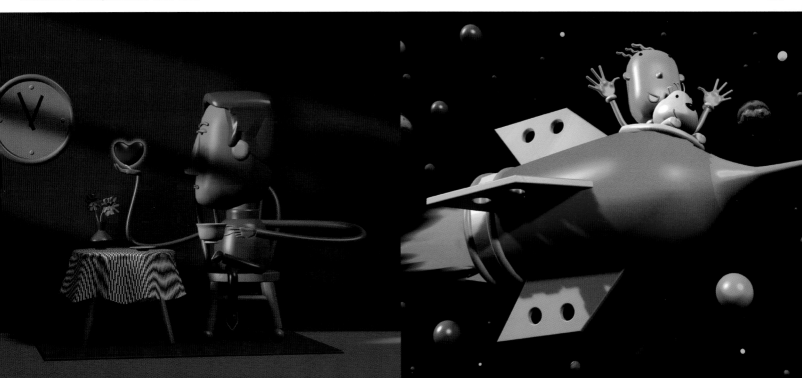

LULU

germany

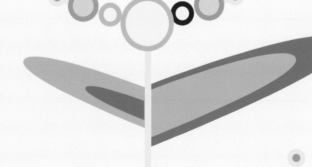

MONIE TRAIN

japan

蹴道君-Syudo Kun

球道君-Kyudo Kun

Marisa
· from Barcelona
· Passionate person

Katarina
· from Geneva
· A dog lover

Hoa
· from Ho Chi Minh
· hobby-Movie appreciation

Laila
· from Kathmandu
· hobby-cricket

concept

All eggs series are manufactured with the egg-shaped ball and the part of each character.

Dolores
· from Los Cabos
· favorite foods-tabasco

Naomi
· from Chicago
· dream-musician

Irina
· from Moscow
· hobby-a ballet

Orivia
· from Buenos Aires
· a horse-riding lover

エココ-Ecoco

蟹江さん-Kanie San

eggs

エコロ-Ecoro

マフィーナ-Mafiena

スペーシー-Spacy

パフォーマン-Performan

パンパン-Panpan

ペンペン-Penpen

プンプン-Punpun

大熊猫団-Ohkumaneko Dan

チャンプ君-Champ Kun

サンちゃん-San Chan

桃太郎-Momotaroh

侍丸-Samuraimaru

王子君-Ohji Kun

フツ子-Futhuko

教授-Kyojyu

サラリー氏-Salarie Si

Afro Ken Plush

DREAM KITTY

canada

japan

korea

Afro Ken Key Chain Plush

AFRO KEN

Afro Ken is a dog that upon first sight leaves a strong impression that you will not forget! Afro Ken is very mysterious - especially in North America.

Afro Ken Toilet Cover

Afro Ken Scarf

Afro Ken Pouf

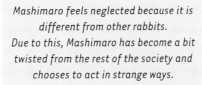

MashiMaro Cushion (L)

MASHI MARO

Mashimaro feels neglected because it is different from other rabbits.
Due to this, Mashimaro has become a bit twisted from the rest of the society and chooses to act in strange ways.

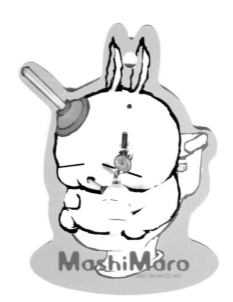

MashiMaro Seat Belt

MashiMaro Handle Cover

KOGEPAN

*Kogepan has gone a little wrong for being made burned.
It's a strange character that can't help saying negative
words like "you will dump me anyway."*

Kogepan Plush

Kogepan Apron

Kogepan Slippers

TARE PANDA

Tarepanda was born totally against the complex digital technology and computer graphics. Its warm and hand-made pencil touch was very unique to be born in the late 90's.

Bath Stopper Chain

Mouse Pad

Comb & Mirror With Bag

Greeting card

Hand Break Cover

Auto Gear Cover

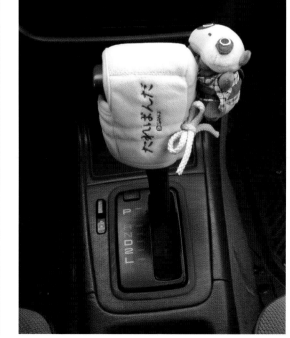

YUKA MORII

japan

SOMETHING FUN, 2003

SOMETHING FUN!

SOMETHING FUN!

YUKA MORII MINI EXHIBITION VOL.2
SOMETHING FUN!

www.yuka-design.com

www. yuka-design .com

www.yuka-design.com

www.yuka-design.com

photo by K.Yamaji

photo by K.Yamaji

photo by K.Yamaji

photo by K.Yamaji

CLAY DESIGN
YUKA DESIGN CO.,LTD.

PHOTO BY KAZUNORI YAMAJI

190   yuka morii

Above left: Cover book / NHK - Above right: Cover Batabata Nurse - Below left: Train Company ADV / Odakyu Company - Below right: Bank Adv / 82 bank

©YUKA MORII

ESSERINI

italy

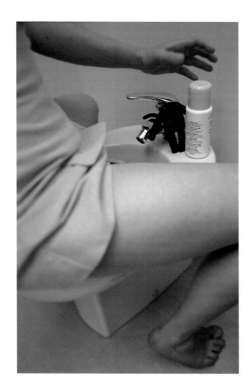

One day, sitting on a train I fell asleep. When I woke up I decided to draw the "ESSERINI".

I drew them while travelling between Bozzolo and Milan, I drew them holding the phone in one hand, I drew them as I was listening to you talking about love troubles.

One afternoon, as I was eating some pasta with tomato sauce, I realised I had to make some kind of rag-dolls using my old sweaters but mostly my leggings which by then had started making me look publicly ridiculous. It was back in the 1980s.

I used buttons to make the eyes, and also beads, those you use to make bracelets.

I chose the most beautiful drawings but also the ugliest and they came to life one by one up to 123 of them. Some "Esserini" are big, others small.

I was astonished then, and I am now, to see how they looked as coming to life from the paper.

Every love chat, every journey by train, the long phone calls which make your ear sweat were magically turning into the "Esserini".

Every "Esserino" has got a stone inside it. I like stones and inside the Esserini a stone acts as heart.

And then one day, when I was already 27 ad I had also given birth to a child, the sun was shining, it wasn't hot, just warm, it was Spring time, I was in the garden sitting on a chair that I had painted yellow and I was very proud of it, I was also wearing a hat, I think...well that day I began writing stories, one for each Esserino, one by one up to 123.

I enjoyed writing those stories. I love stories, I enjoy both listening to story-telling and telling stories myself, especially if they are true stories, but if trey are made up it's the same.

Every Esserino has got its own personality, every Esserino has chosen its own human being. I like them.

Un giorno seduta sopra al treno, mi sono addormentata.

Poi mi sono svegliata e ho deciso di disegnare gli esserini.

Li ho disegnati durante molti viaggi tra bozzolo e milano, li ho disegnati con la cornetta del telefono in mano, li ho disegnati mentre ti ascoltavo parlare di problemi sentimentali.

Un pomeriggio stavo mangiando un piatto di penne al sugo e ho capito che dovevo fare dei pupazzi in stoffa con i miei vecchi maglioni, ma soprattutto con le panta calze che ormai cominciavano a rendermi ridicola in pubblico. Erano gli anni '80.

Ho usato i bottoni per fare gli occhi, ma anche dei corallini, quelli che si usano per fare i braccialetti.

Ho preso i disegni più belli, ma anche i più brutti e sono nati uno ad uno fino ad arrivare a 123, alcuni esserini sono grandi, altri piccoli.

Mi stupivo e ancora mi stupisco, di come fossero uguali ai disegni e di come sembravano staccarsi dai fogli, e tutti i discorsi sentimentali, i viaggi in treno, le telefonate lunghissime che fanno sudare l'orecchio si trasformavano magicamente in esserini.

Ogni esserino ha dentro un sasso.

Mi piacciono i sassi, e dentro agli esserini fanno il cuore.

Poi un giorno quando ormai avevo già 27 anni e avevo partorito anche un bambino, c'era un bel sole, ma non c'era caldo, era primavera, ero in giardino ed ero seduta sopra ad una sedia che avevo dipinto di giallo, di cui andavo molto fiera, avevo in testa anche un cappello, credo, ho iniziato a scrivere delle storie, una per ogni esserino, una ad una fino a 123.

Mi piaceva scrivere quelle storie lì.

Mi piacciono le storie, mi piace quando qualcuno me le racconta, e mi piace raccontarle, soprattutto se sono storie vere o finte è lo stesso.

Ogni esserino ha una sua personalità, ogni esserino ha preso la sua strada, ha scelto il suo umano, a me piacciono.

n. 32

YOU NEED LOVE
TO TAKE AND GIVE?
WITHOUT ME YOU CANNOT LIVE
esserino for those who fear dogs

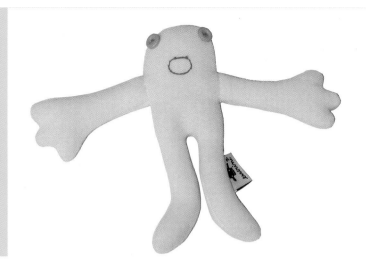

To be: be **is** used to represent some aspects of what **is** considered reality; to express the essence or the primeval apparition; everything which has some kind of life or existence in itself.
To **be** or not to **be**.
God **is**, God **is** not.
Don't worry about what **is** not.
One must take life as it **is**.
Let there **be** light and there **was** light.
There **are** no perfect men.
Nobody **is** naive.
Once upon a time there **was**…
What will I **be**?
What's the matter now?
Let it **be**.
Here we **are**!
Are you there?
I don't know where I **am**.
I'll get married when I **am** old.
Don't take him into account, he **is** just a broke!
Human **beings.**
Beings from outer space.

Esserino: little being, baby, little creature, any living being that stirs up feelings of tenderness and sympathy.

n. 118

TAKE A FAST RIDE
AT HIGH SPEED,
IF IT'S HAPPINESS YOU NEED
esserino for those
who feel like teenagers

n. 68

THE MOST BEAUTIFUL
WORLDWIDE, IF YOU KEEP
HIM BY YOUR SIDE
esserino for those who
need love

n. 42

LET HIM IN YOUR HEAD AND INSIDE
A PARTY WILL EXPLODE INTO LIFE

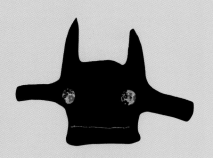

Essere
esprimere, possedere, rappresentare
un qualche aspetto di quella che
è considerata la realtà. Esprimere
essenza o apparizione primordiale,
ciò che ha una qualunque forma di
vita, di esistenza:

Dio è, Dio non è; non preoccupatevi
per ciò che non è, bisogna prendere
la vita com'è; e la luce fu
Non ci sono uomini perfetti, non c'è
nessuno che sia così ingenuo
C'era una volta
Sarà quel che sarà
Quel che è stato è stato
Che sarà di me?
Che cosa c'è adesso?
Così sia
Ci siamo!
Ci sei?
Non so dove sono
Mi sposerò quando sarò vecchio
Gli esseri viventi
Sei un ammirevole odioso
Non farci caso è un povero

Esserino diminutivo
Bambinello, creaturina, essere
animato che ispira tenerezza e
compassione:
povero esserino muore dal freddo

n. 106

ALWAYS POLISHED, SMART AND HIGH.
THERE'S NO NEED
TO JOIN THE FIGHT
esserino for those who suffer from
dizziness

n. 80

THERE IS NOTHING LIKE
STRATEGIC,
ALL THAT HAPPENS IS
JUST MAGIC
esserino for
important decisions

n. 51

LITTLE KNOWING IS
TRUE LOVING
esserino for those who
know what's what

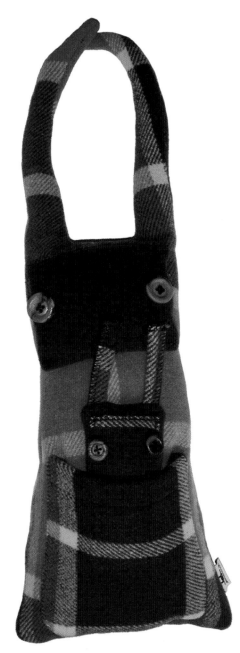

n. 122

YOU GAVE IT ALL
AND HAD YOUR SHARE,
NOW YOU HAVE A FRUIT
TO BEAR
esserino for the
mothers, in every sense

n. 86

BY THE MAGIC OF A WITCH, YOU MEET FRIEN-
DS ACROSS THE BRIDGE
esserino to believe in dreams

n. 66

ALL SEEMS CLEAR JUST LIKE STRIPPED
BARE, BUT YOUR HEART STAYS UNAWARE
esserino to change life

n. 112

BOGEY KEEPS YOU AWAKE AT NIGHT? HOLD
ME CLOSE TO YOUR HEART TIGHT
esserino for those who fear everything

n. 103

ON THE BELLY THERE'S A FACE:
GIVES YOUR HEAD A PERFECT PLACE
esserino to feel

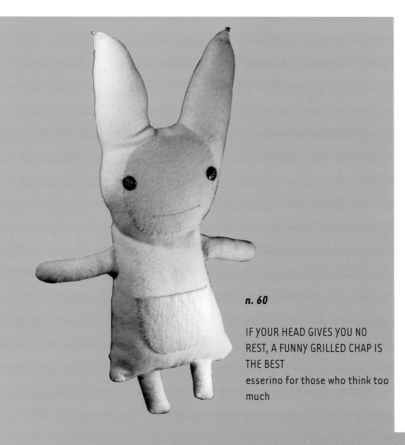

n. 60

IF YOUR HEAD GIVES YOU NO
REST, A FUNNY GRILLED CHAP IS
THE BEST
esserino for those who think too
much

n. 100

YOU FEEL LOST AND WITH
NO CLUE, TAKE ME ON
AND I'LL LOVE YOU
esserino for those who
can endlessly love

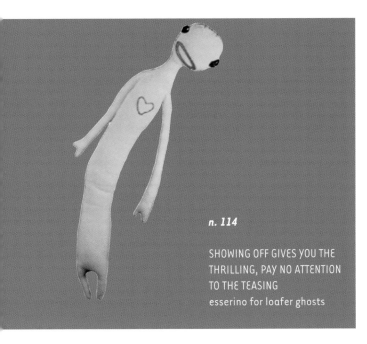

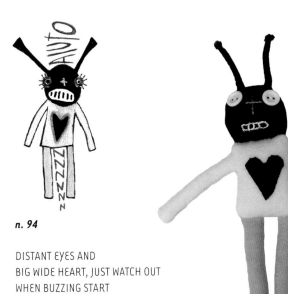

n. 114

SHOWING OFF GIVES YOU THE
THRILLING, PAY NO ATTENTION
TO THE TEASING
esserino for loafer ghosts

n. 94

DISTANT EYES AND
BIG WIDE HEART, JUST WATCH OUT
WHEN BUZZING START
esserino for the shy

n. 64

AN ENIGMA YOU'VE GONE THROUGH,
DON'T MAKE GIBLETS OUT OF YOU
esserino for those who get lost

n. 116

GREED OF FEELINGS SENSE
ECLIPSE, LOVING WORDS BETWEEN
YOUR LIPS
esserino for the too serious

DELICATESSEN

italy

LADY FRAGOLA

RAVANELLI

AGLIETTO

CAROTINA

PICCOLA MELANZANA

FUNGHETTO

MASTER POMODORO

VECCHIA CIPOLLA

PEPERONCINO

LADY FRAGOLA

POMODORO

CAROTINA

PEPERONCINO

CAROTINA

VECCHIA CIPOLLA

CAROTINA

RAVANELLI

AGLIETTO

PICCOLA MELANZANA

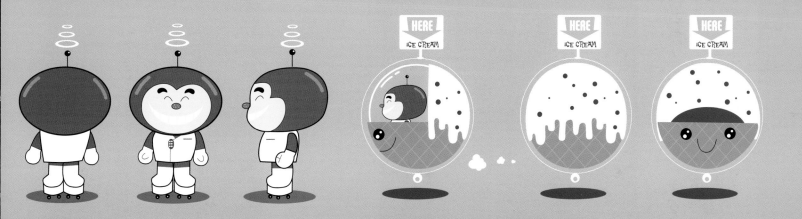

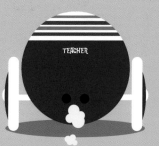

the teacher
age: 26
height: 176cm - weight: 64kg
Job: English teach of Junior
High school
Characteristic: Seriously.
Don't laugh all the time.
He is the tenant of this family.

the uncle
age: 36
height: 172cm - weight:86kg
Job: Ice cream peddler
Characteristic: Straight,
honest.

the father
age: 45
height: 210cm - weight: 72kg
Job: Bodyguard or spy etc.
Characteristic: easy to be
nervous in some circumstances.

the mother
age: 38
height: 160 cm - weight 80 kg
Job: Soft drinking seller
but part time job ....etc
Characteristic: Enthusiasm,
traditional woman, kindness.

the older sister
age: 17
height: 168cm - weight: 50kg
Job: Senior High
Characteristic: Fashion, Egypt is
her favorite. She can't get along
with her mother and don't wanna be the one like her mother.

the brother
age: 12
height: 140cm weight: 38kg
Job: Junior High
Characteristic : wear heavy glasses and heavy bag. Passion. Sunny boy.

the younger sister
age: 8
height: 122cm weight: 25kg
Job: Elementary school
Characteristic : Blue (sometimes), Crying all the time.

the cousin
age: 5
height: 110cm weight: 18 kg
Job: Kindergarten
Characteristic: Like crowd. Don't wanna be alone. Childish.

the pet

the grand ma
age: 68
height: 155cm weight: 45kg
Job: housewife
Characteristic: Kindness, lovely, childish.

the grand pa
age: 70
height: 165cm weight: 50kg
Job Prefecture, or local leader
Characteristic : To get half the result with twice the effort, but enthusiasm.

GENEVIEVE GAUCKLER
1967
17 Avenue Trudaine
75009 Paris - France
www.g2works.com
genevieve@g2works.com

BORIS HOPPEK
1970
www.borishoppek.de
hoppek@web.de

MEOMI DESIGN
-
833 W.62nd Avenue
Vancouver BC
V6P 2E3 Canada
www.meomi.com
info@meomi.com

TINO
1968
6bis rue déserte
67000 strasbourg - france
www.tinoland.com
tino@tinoland.com
Tino is represented by agent 002
Perrine Dorin - perrine@agent002.com
www.agent002.com

JEAN-MARIE ANGLES
1964
36 Rue des Rigoles
75020 Paris - France
www.adn23.com/jmangles/
j-m.angles@wanadoo.fr
Jean marie Angles is represented by Illustrissimo.
Michel Lagarde - michel@illustrissimo.com
www.illustrissimo.com

YUKIO KUWAJIMA
Royal Chateau-202 3-13-14
Itabashi-ku Tokyo
Japan 175-0092
www.lovemonkey.jp
kuwajima@pop01.odn.ne.jp

DOUDOUBOY
1976
2 rue Rathgeber
67100 Strasbourg - France
http://doudouboy.free.fr
doudouboy@noos.fr

NATSUKO KOGURE
1967
2-21-36-206,Kouya,Ichikawa City
2720013 Chibaken Japan
www.asahi-net.or.jp/~TH4K-MYS/kogure/kogure.html
YHB02327@nifty.com

KEN HOSHINO
1969
10-6, Kitabayashi Shinbayashi-cho,
Chiryu-shi, Aichi, 472-0017 Japan
www.tcp-ip.or.jp/~kenken/
kenken@tcp-ip.or.jp

FREDERIC PÈAULT
1970
99 Av Parmentier
75011 Paris - France
www.illustronaute.com
info@fred-peault.com

PACO AGUAYO
1976
Arrecife 2577
Colonia Santa Edwiges
44580 Guadalajara, Jalisco.
México
www.haiku.com.mx/monos/
paco@haiku.com.mx

KANAE ASAI
1962
3-1-11-803 Ikebukuro Tosimaku
Tokyo Japan 171-0014
www.jade.dti.ne.jp/~asai
asai@jade.dti.ne.jp

LA PATAMODELEUSE
JOSEPHINE PUJOS
1979
Rue des Peupliers, 36
75013 Paris - France
www.mixeurgraphic.com
www.lapatamodeleuse.com/
josephine@lapatamodeleuse.com

NICOLA
Rie Sugihara
Shinohara Higashi 1-6-25-206
Kouhoku-ku, Yokohama City,
Kanagawa prefecture 222-0022
nicola@syd.odn.ne.jp

SATOMI YAI
-
4-1-105 Nampeidai
Myamae-ku, Kawasaki-shi
Kanagawa-ken, Japan
www10.plala.or.jp/deinto/live_in/live_coun.html
woopie@vmail.plala.or.jp

D'HOLBACHIE-YOKO
1971
5-223-803, Yamamoto-cho, Naka-ku,
2310851 Yokohama-shi, Kanagawa-ken, Japan
www.dholbachie.com
yoko@dhoibachie.com

IAN STOKES
csero interactive
1147 West Ohio St #402
Chicago Illinois 60622
USA
www.csero.com
ianstokes@ameritech.net

HIROSHI YOSHII
1962
#304, 1-2-13 Tamagawadai, Setagayaku, Tokyo
1580096 Japan
www.yoshii.com
hiroshi@yoshii.com

MAMIKO HASEBE
1974
3-501 Ageo-house, 2-82-2 Nishimiyashita,
Ageo-shi, Saitama-Ken,
362-0043 Japan
http://home8.highway.ne.jp/mmk
mmk@ph.highway.ne.jp

RAFAEL MENDOZA
Pichilingue, 42 Col. Marte
México, 08830 D.F.
http://rafamendoza.com
luzazul1@prodigy.net.mx
Rafael Mendoza is represented by estudio 002
Isabelle fanton - isabelle@estudio002.com
www.estudio002.com

LULU
1977
stargarderstrasse 32 - 10437 Berlin - Germany
www.plasticpirate.com
lulu@plasticpirate.com
Delicatessen is represented by
KATE LARKWORTHY ARTIST REPRESENTATION, LTD
www.larkworthy.com - kate@larkworthy.com

MONIE TRAIN
takeshi kitagawa - 1975
ai toyoshima -1973
4-8-28-402,Nakamura-kita,
Nerima-ku,Tokyo 176-0023 - Japan
www.d5.dion.ne.jp/~monie-t
monie-t@d5.dion.ne.jp

DREAMKITTY
-
23 Gartshore Drive
Whitby, ON L1P 1N7
Canada
www.dreamkitty.com

EMMA
1972
1-3-4-605 seishin-cho edogawa-ku tokyo
 134-0087 japan
http://member.nifty.ne.jp/
emma@mbf.nifty.com

YUKA MORII
1965
2-33-1, iriya, taito-ku,
110-0013 Tokyo, Japan
http://yuka-design.com
yuka@yuka-design.com

ESSERINI
Simona Costanzo - 1969
Str. Langhirano, 443/A
43010 Corcagnano Parma - Italy
www.esserini.it
info@esserini.it

DELICATESSEN
gabriele fantuzzi -1967
cristiana valentini -1970
via che guevara 55,
42100 Reggio Emilia, Italy
www.delicatessen.it
info@delica.it

Delicatessen is represented in Europe (except UK)
by Illustrissimo
Michel Lagarde - michel@illustrissimo.com
www.illustrissimo.com

Delicatessen is represented in America+UK+Japan by
KATE LARKWORTHY ARTIST REPRESENTATION, LTD
182 Norfolk Street #3 New York 10002
www.larkworthy.com
kate@larkworthy.com

Thanks to:
Matteo Bittanti
Genevieve Gauckler
Meomi Design
Jean-Marie Angles
Doudouboy
Ken Hoshino
Paco Aguayo
Josephine Pujos
Boris Hoppek
Tinoland
Yukio Kuwajima
Natsuko Kogure
Frederic Pèault
Nicola
Kanae Asai
Satomi Yai
D'holbachie Yoko
Hiroshi Yoshii
Ian Stokes
Mamiko Hasebe
Rafael Mendoza
Lulu
Monie Train
Dreamkitty.com
Emma
Yuka Morii
Esserini
Fabio Caleffi +
Happy Books staff
and all the family of
Mondofragile

illustration:
Mamiko Hasebe